The Elizabethan Theatre V

The Elizabethan Theatre V

Papers given at the Fifth International
Conference on Elizabethan Theatre held at the
University of Waterloo, Ontario, in July 1973

Edited and with an introduction by
G. R. HIBBARD
Department of English,
University of Waterloo

Published in collaboration with the
University of Waterloo

Archon Books

PN
2589
I5
1973

Published in Canada by the Macmillan Company
of Canada Limited and simultaneously
published in the United States of America as an
Archon Book by The Shoe String Press, Inc.,
Hamden, Connecticut.

Printed in Canada

Library of Congress Cataloging in Publication Data

International Conference on Elizabethan Theatre, 5th,
University of Waterloo, 1973. The Elizabethan theatre V.

Includes bibliographical references.
1. Theater — England — History — Congresses. 2. English
drama — Early modern and Elizabethan, 1500-1600 — History
and criticism — Congresses. I. Hibbard, George Richard. II.
Title.

PN2589.15   1973   792'.0942   75-14300
ISBN 0-208-01515-9

This book has been published with the help of a grant
from the Humanities Research Council of Canada,
using funds provided by the Canada Council.

Acknowledgments

The holding of the Fifth International Conference on Elizabethan Theatre at the University of Waterloo in July 1973, and the publication now of the papers that were read at the conference, afford, between them, a pleasant and highly appropriate instance of cooperative effort at four different levels: the international, the federal, the provincial and the local. The main burden of sustaining the conference itself was borne by the Ministry of Education for Ontario, acting through its Department for Cultural Exchanges. The generous grant provided by the Ministry was the indispensable foundation on which the conference rested. Strong support also came from the British Council, which supplied the travel grant for Dr. Richard Southern, and from the University of Waterloo, in the form of cash and services. The publication of the papers was made possible by a subvention from the Humanities Research Council of Canada enabling the Macmillan Company of Canada to continue an association with the conference that it has had from the beginning.

In none of these cases was the help restricted to the provision of money. The director of a conference such as this applies for financial assistance to a Ministry, a Council or a similar body; but he actually talks to or corresponds with individuals. In every case, I met with understanding and encouragement.

A special word of thanks is due to those who gave far more of their time and effort to the conference than could reasonably be expected of them, and to those who worked for its success on a purely voluntary basis. In addition to seeing this volume through the press, Mrs. Diane Mew, of the Macmillan Company of Canada, attended every meeting of the conference, leaving its members in no doubt about her deep personal interest in its proceedings. Professor Gerald M. Newman contributed a series of taped performances to illustrate some Twentieth-Century Approaches to

Acknowledgments

the Production of the Mystery Play. At very short notice, Professor Clifford Leech put together a most entertaining informal address, in the shape of a "spoof" lecture, to bring the conference to a hilarious close. Finally, six graduate students – Jim Andersen, Kate Andersen, Jane Britton, Edy Rice, Susan Steele and Frances Timleck – working together as a very efficient and good-humoured team, saw to it that things ran smoothly and with a minimum of fuss. They were invaluable.

The chapter from Dr. Richard Southern's recent book, *The Staging of Plays before Shakespeare*, is included by kind permission of the publishers, Messrs. Faber and Faber; and Dr. Southern himself generously provided the design for the book jacket.

The index was compiled by Frances Timleck.

G.R.H.

Contents

Introduction

For those who acted in its earliest productions *The Taming of the Shrew* probably had a personal application and a special interest that no modern presentation of the play can possibly hope to recapture. Unlike the players who appear so opportunely at Elsinore, the troupe that arrives at the home of the nameless Lord in the Induction to the comedy simply turns up there. No news of their coming has preceded them, no preparation has been made for their reception. Nevertheless, they are given "friendly welcome every one" and led off to the buttery. Then, suitably refreshed, they proceed to put on their play for the entertainment of the metamorphosed tinker and his "wife," who sit "aloft" to watch it. The stage (assuming that *The Taming of the Shrew* was first shown in a London theatre) has become the great hall of an Elizabethan country house; and the actors are engaged in playing what many of them had, in all likelihood, been doing in sober earnest not very long before, and were, no doubt, to do often enough again. Reading or viewing the Induction, one is tempted to conclude that Shakespeare, anticipating Dr. Richard Southern and other modern historians of the theatre, is pointing to a close relationship between the great hall and the public stage. Nor is this the sum of what the Induction has to tell us. Before it is over, we have also been given reason to think that there may well be some intimate connections between "a pleasant comedy," "a Christmas gambold," "a tumbling-trick" and "a kind of history." Sly's notions about the antecedents of "festive comedy" tally remarkably well with Dr. C. L. Barber's.

It is clear that Shakespeare's first-hand knowledge of the theatre and of other playing places was one of his greatest assets as a practising dramatist. Equally important for his success was his profound sense of belonging to a tradition. Unlike Marlowe, he does not dismiss the efforts of his predecessors as the "jigging veins of riming mother wits." He makes fun of their absurdities, of

ix

course, and glorious fun it is; but his parodies are always done with affection, and neither in *Love's Labour's Lost* nor in *A Midsummer Night's Dream* does he allow the amateur actors to be put down by the scoffs of the courtiers before whom they perform. Exploring the potentialities of his heritage in another and more serious fashion, he transmutes the old Vice of the interludes into Richard III and, ultimately, into Iago, makes *Measure for Measure* out of George Whetstone's *Promos and Cassandra*, and converts *The Famous Victories of Henry V* into the Two Parts of *Henry IV* and *Henry V*. His art transcends that of his forerunners to such an extent that it seems to belong to another order of things altogether, yet its foundations are solidly based on the achievements of the past.

Recognition of this fact would in itself demand that a conference which devotes itself to the study of the Elizabethan theatre, in the widest sense of that term, should at some stage in its existence turn its attention to the pre-Shakespearian theatre. Interestingly enough, however, the decision to hold a conference on this particular topic came out of a conference that was concerned primarily not with Shakespeare but with Ben Jonson. At first sight Jonson seems a rather improbable sire for such an offspring; but, as soon as one thinks about the matter, the improbability disappears. After all, avowed and self-proclaimed classicist though he was, he very soon discovered that his roots were firmly fixed in his native soil and, acting on this discovery, he carefully revised *Every Man in His Humour* in order to change it from a pseudo-Florentine into an authentic Londoner. His blank verse derives from Marlowe's; his plots are multiple rather than single; and, above all, both his overt didacticism and his innate delight in cleverness and trickery, coupled with his scorn for folly and stupidity, drew him irresistibly towards the morality play and the interlude. In 1599, as the author of *Every Man Out of His Humour*, he used the words *Vetus Comoedia* to describe the Old Comedy of the Greeks, but twenty years later, when speaking to Drummond of Hawthornden about *The Devil is an Ass*, he applied the same term to the drama of his own country in the late fifteenth and early sixteenth centuries.

Both Shakespeare and Jonson, then, are aware of and bear witness to the continuity of their own work with the plays of the past in England, and they do so despite the fact that they themselves wrote for theatres such as had not existed prior to 1576: buildings designed for the specific purpose of showing plays. The erection of The Theatre and the opening of the Blackfriars were indeed climactic events in the history of the drama, an open and explicit acknowledgment that this form of entertainment had become fully professional. But both the building of the one house and the conversion of the other were undertaken to meet the needs of companies of players that were already in being and to cater for the tastes, the interests and the convenience of an existing body of spectators. The players, those who wrote for them, and those who came to watch and to listen to them were the true foundation on which the Elizabethan theatre was raised.

Such being the case, it follows that the ultimate goal of enquiry for those who are interested in the Elizabethan theatre must be "To find the pleyers and all that longeth therto," as R. W. Ingram so admirably puts it in a paper printed in this volume. It is clearly an unattainable goal. We do not know, and it seems highly unlikely that we ever shall know, how, when or where "playing" began in England. As for "all that longeth therto," it is plainly beyond the wit of man, extending, as it does, from such imponderables as the substantive text of *Hamlet* and the precise shape and structure of the Globe Theatre at the one end to such apparent trivia as "a leather pilch" or "a little bladder of vinegar prickt" at the other. Yet, unattainable though the goal may be, we do at least know that patience and intelligence, properly applied, will serve to bring us closer to it. Those last two little items – Dekker's description of the player's garb as he trudged beside his play-waggon along the highway, and Thomas Preston's stage direction for injecting some verisimilitude into a stage murder without imperilling the life of the actor – illustrate how much incidental information is to be found within the plays themselves. Under the guidance of Sir Walter Greg we have learned how useful stage directions can be as an indication of the kind of manuscript that the printer of a play was working from. Now we are coming to appreciate their value as pointers to the physical features of the acting area that a play was designed for.

Patience is needed to collect these scraps of evidence, and their interpretation requires a trained intelligence. But it is the larger questions so intimately bound up with these lesser matters, questions about development, continuity, innovation, tradition and so forth that demand the greatest wariness and the unremitting exercise of searching scepticism. Once upon a time, and not so very long ago either, many of us had a nice, clear picture in our minds of the growth of English drama. It began in the church and it was written in Latin. Then the plays were translated into the vernacular and acted in the streets. A process of secularization had thus begun; and that process led, in due course, to the flowering of the drama in the late sixteenth century. It was all very neat and eminently satisfactory, because it was so intelligible and so elegant. Similarly, we thought there had been such a thing as *the* Elizabethan theatre, an ideal pattern to which each individual theatre of the time either conformed entirely or sought to conform. We knew, or thought we knew, exactly what that theatre looked like, and we were confident that an inner stage was an indispensable and integral part of it. Today both these beautiful constructions lie in ruins. Thirty-five years or so of ever-increasing enquiry, involving the adducing of new evidence, the re-examination of old evidence and, above all, the rejection of the idea of progress, has left them in much the same state that the Three Unities were in after Dr. Johnson had considered the basic assumptions on which they rested.

The International Conference on Elizabethan Theatre has played its part both in the necessary work of destruction and in the even more necessary work of reconstruction which is now taking place. Introducing the volume that contained the papers read at the first conference, held in 1968, David Galloway remarked that the main emphasis of the proceedings had been on the need to re-examine and to revise "certain traditional preconceptions about Elizabethan theatres in general," adding that it "became clearer and clearer as the sessions went on that these revisions were likely to be radical." The same spirit animated the conference of 1973, where the constant exchange of ideas which is so essential to all revision was stimulated by a series of fortunate coincidences. By design the papers were read in an order that respected the claims of chronology, but it was not by design that they fell into complementary pairs, so that a wide sweep by one speaker was followed immediately by a piece of close and detailed analysis from another, or some queries about the staging of one play prepared the way for a consideration of the literary values of another.

The very title of the opening paper, "Discontinuities in Medieval Acting Traditions," set the tone for much that was to follow. In it David Bevington endorses the views of those who have perceived strong Darwinian assumptions behind the general notions about medieval drama that were current until some twenty years ago, and who have challenged the idea that the cycle drama evolved directly out of the drama of the church. He then goes on to attack Glynne Wickham's theory that the corresponding shift from the use of clerical actors to the use of lay actors was gradual and co-operative, arguing that in church drama there is no solid evidence that the acting ever moved beyond a very rudimentary level. The probabilities are, he suggests, that the main parts were sustained by men, and that it was the demands of music, rather than of theatre, that determined the casting. Cycle drama, on the other hand, was much more innovative, following no set pattern either in casting or in staging. Different towns worked out different solutions to the problems that faced them, including, on occasions, a recourse to the employment of professional actors to sustain some of the major roles. Holding that the extent of professionalism in late medieval drama has very likely been underestimated, he concludes by demonstrating the necessary links between professionalism and the practice of touring, which, in its turn, led on to the creation of "a truly popular theatre."

Early in his paper, David Bevington asks some pertinent questions. Among them are these: "Who are these actors? Are they professionals or amateurs? Do they employ boys and women?" While those questions were still fresh in the minds of the audience R. W. Ingram proceeded to supply some of the answers. His paper, " 'To find the pleyers and all that longeth therto,' " deals with the extensive material that has survived about the Cappers' Company in Coventry which was responsible for the production of the pageant-play of *The Resurrection*, *The Harrowing of Hell* and *The Meeting with the Maries*. Beginning with an account of the way in which the Cappers financed their play, Professor Ingram then moves on to the fascinating topic of the versatile Robert Crow, whose name appears in all the records that are extant for the period from 1510 to 1566. Playwright, actor, maker and handler of properties, Crow was either a man of many parts or more than one man. Professor Ingram inclines to the latter view, but refuses to commit himself on the question of how many more than one.

What he does show quite conclusively is that the plays at Coventry underwent fairly frequent revision and that the actors in them were not all men, since there was a role for "the lettell chyld" during the period from 1549 to 1579.

At the time when the conference was held, Dr. Richard Southern's most recent book, *The Staging of Plays before Shakespeare*, had just been published in England but was not yet available in North America. He therefore regaled his audience with a summary of its main line of argument. Like the interluders who were his theme, he entered the hall and staged a show on the floor of it. Armed with a piece of chalk, which he wielded as though it were Prospero's wand, he began with a sketch of the hall of a sixteenth-century house. Then, as he quoted and enacted one significant stage direction after another, he added detail on detail to that original sketch, until some final flourishes, that were not without their dash of legerdemain, transformed it into a sketch of the Fortune Theatre. The theory was plain for all to see. Both because it was a summary and because it was an unscripted performance rather than a lecture, Dr. Southern's talk could not be reproduced in this volume. Instead, he has modified for us and allowed us to print the chapter on *Apius and Virginia* (c. 1560) from his book. This play, he considers, marks a crucial moment in the development of the drama in England because it requires a "scaffold" for its staging. Hitherto, the interluders had made an apparently spontaneous incursion into the hall, using the floor of it as their acting area. But a stage, no matter how elementary it may be, is something that has to be constructed and placed in position before the play can start; it stares the spectator in the eye and tells him what he is in for. The pretence of spontaneity can no longer be sustained. The Interlude, in the old sense of that word, is already on its death-bed.

But, while the Interlude was on its way out in the sixties and seventies, the most dynamic figure in it certainly was not. Ingenious, unscrupulous and infinitely adaptable from his beginnings, the Vice changed with the changing times, as J. A. B. Somerset neatly reminds us with the title of his paper, " 'Fair is foul and foul is fair': Vice-Comedy's Development and Theatrical Effects." Believing that the morality play underwent a constant process "of change, experiment, and commitment," especially during the years 1480 to 1540, he strongly rejects the notion that the comic element in it is either intended to supply relief or exists solely to be condemned. In his view, the main source of the morality was not the idea of a psychomachia but the picture of life as a pilgrimage. In the course of his journey, man is exposed to and beset by temptation; and his seduction by it will only become dramatically convincing if the temptation is presented in such a way as to be truly attractive. Thus ambiguity arises. The vices, and later the Vice, have to be both evil and comic. They must entertain the hero, and hence the audience. The condition of their success is a sense of the theatre; and it is this sense of the theatre that ensures the Vice's survival. Perhaps Darwin was not so far out after all.

The first four papers are all concerned with and confine themselves to questions and issues that lie on the farther side of the critical year 1576. The last four take up the story after that date. Following in the footsteps of Granville Barker, and preferring the empirical method to the theoretical, T. W. Craik goes back to the original texts of several pre-Shakespearian plays, and to the stage directions in those texts, in an effort to determine what a sixteenth-century audience might have seen when these plays were first put on. His paper, "The Reconstruction of Stage Action from Early Dramatic Texts," opens with a consideration of some of the problems George Peele faced the players with in his *David and Bethsabe*. It then turns its attention to some of the puzzles in the last scene of *The Spanish Tragedy* – a topic that was to be pursued further by D. F. Rowan later in the proceedings – and goes on to argue that any direction which calls for the employment of an upper acting area in the staging of *Dr. Faustus* is highly suspect. Marlowe proves, in fact, to be extremely fertile in creating the kind of difficulties for the actors that excite Professor Craik's interest; and the paper offers some attractive solutions to such matters as the ownership of the staff with which Jacomo "kills" the dead Barnardine in *The Jew of Malta* and what happens to the spit that is prepared for the murder of Edward II.

Peter Saccio takes up a puzzle of another kind, though problems of setting and staging enter into it. Admitting that when he wrote his book on Lyly's court comedies he found it impossible to fit *Endimion* into either of the two main groups – the static and the narrative – into which the rest of the court comedies fitted so neatly, he seeks to answer the question: what sort of play is

Endimion? The answer he arrives at is implicit in the title of his paper, "The Oddity of Lyly's *Endimion.*" He notes that in this play Lyly "modifies or departs from his usual practices in setting, in characterization, and in the kinds of action chosen for presentation." The place is indefinite, and there are curious features even about something so apparently specific as the "lunary bank" on which the hero sleeps his long sleep. There is a strange and uncharacteristic lack of particularity in some of the characters, and especially in Cynthia. Moreover, this comedy does not adhere to one mode of action, but switches from patterned design, Lyly's favourite manner, to romantic narrative, and back again. Taking all these unusual qualities into account, the paper arrives at the satisfactory conclusion that the comedy is like a dream, and is meant to be seen as a dream.

When the first Conference on Elizabethan Theatre was held at Waterloo in 1968, D. F. Rowan read a fascinating paper on the drawings by Inigo Jones for the remodelled Cockpit-in-Court. A year later, at the second conference, he followed his first paper up with another concerning the significance of some other drawings in the Worcester College collection. It was, therefore, peculiarly fitting that at the fifth conference, which was characterized by that *discordia concors* so admired by the Renaissance, he should apply his knowledge of the Elizabethan theatre to a specific problem: "The Staging of *The Spanish Tragedy.*" Like T. W. Craik, with whom, incidentally, he agrees about the vexed question of the throwing down of the key in the final scene, he goes back for enlightenment to the original stage directions. These lead him to conclude that the Ghost and Revenge should sit on the main stage, not "above." His main concern, however, is with the "arbour" – what it was, where it was, and the various uses it could be put to. He emphasizes, and with every justification, the importance which this particular property has in the play, and makes a most ingenious suggestion about the way in which it could have been employed in the great *coup de théâtre* at the end.

It is impossible to imagine a more appropriate conclusion to the week's proceedings than that provided by Dr. Inga-Stina Ewbank's paper, " 'What words, what looks, what wonders?': Language and Spectacle in the Theatre of George Peele." Running like a thread through all that had been said hitherto there had been the recognition, sometimes tacit, sometimes overt, but always present, that plays exist to be played, that they are written for performance. Now this assumption was fully articulated. Dr. Ewbank thinks that Peele's achievement has been underrated because his critics have paid too much attention to his words and too little to the other components of the theatrical experience he has to offer. Drama appeals to the eye as well as to the ear, making its effect on the spectator through a conjunction of what is heard and what is seen. She argues that the main purpose Peele had in mind was to create a sense of wonder in his audience, whether it be wonder at the beauty of Bethsabe or wonder at the wickedness of Muly Mahamet, and that he made an extensive and intelligent use of spectacle in order to attain this end. In other words, he brought his experience as a writer of pageants with him to the theatre. There are occasions in his plays when the words amount to little more than a kind of verbal pointing, telling the audience what to look at and how to look at it; but, at his best, Peele can fuse the aural with the visual in such a way as to give a sense of "raptness." This fusion is at its most evident in *The Arraignment of Paris* and in *David and Bethsabe*, a play which she regards as "a link between the Mysteries and Shakespeare's last plays."

As well as talking about plays, members of the conference saw some performances. During the course of the week they went to Stratford on three occasions for productions of *Pericles, The Taming of the Shrew, Othello* and, depending on choice, either *She Stoops to Conquer* or *A Month in the Country*. Nor does this end the tale. Those who were able to stay for the dinner on the last night were entertained by a delightful *jeu d'esprit* from Clifford Leech on the subject of Christ Figures in Shakespeare. Another link between the Mysteries and Shakespeare's last plays?

G. R. Hibbard
Department of English
University of Waterloo

Discontinuity in Medieval Acting Traditions

DAVID BEVINGTON

Fifty years or so ago, a common assumption about medieval drama was that it evolved steadily and progressively toward the secular art of the Renaissance. E. K. Chambers, Karl Young, J. M. Manly and others argued that drama of the church evolved first into drama performed outside the church and then into drama performed in the town, by craft guilds.[1] Concurrently, the argument went, translation into the vernacular provided dramatic texts dealing with biblical history that needed only to be collected and slightly ampliled in order to create the Corpus Christi cycles. The introduction of comedy was viewed as a relatively late phenomenon and part of the process of "secularization" by which medieval drama moved toward the future greatness of the Elizabethan theatre. Medieval plays were read as "Specimens of the Pre-Shaksperean drama," to borrow the memorably fatuous phrase used by Manly for his anthology of medieval drama.

The corrective trend of the last twenty years, spearheaded by F. M. Salter in his *Medieval Drama at Chester*,[2] has insisted on viewing medieval plays as sophisticated literary works in their own right. Along with this insistence has come a sharply revised interpretation of the concept of evolution. O. B. Hardison, in his *Christian Rite and Christian Drama in the Middle Ages*, has incisively demonstrated the Darwinian assumptions governing the point of view of even such critically perceptive men as Chambers

1. E. K. Chambers, *The Mediaeval Stage*, 2 vols. (Oxford, 1903); Karl Young, *The Drama of the Medieval Church*, 2 vols. (Oxford, 1933); and J. M. Manly, ed., *Specimens of the Pre-Shaksperean Drama*, 2 vols. (Boston, 1897).
2. F. M. Salter, *Medieval Drama at Chester* (Toronto, 1955).

and Young.[3] As children of the Protestant Whig-Liberal tradition, they unavoidably viewed the Renaissance as the beginning of the modern period culminating in Victorian Great Britain and her empire; hence, medieval drama was to be seen as a happy prologue to the swelling act, a process of early experiment in which simplest forms presumably came first and developed into more complex forms. As Hardison shows, the obsession with progressive development leads Young, for example, to arrange his monumental two-volume study of the *Drama of the Medieval Church* in patently non-chronological order so that the presupposed movement from Easter drama to Christmas drama and from simple Shepherds' plays to complex Magi plays could be seen more clearly. Hardison's own reassessment of chronology shows that the introduction of the vernacular came remarkably early (in the twelfth-century Anglo-Norman *Adam*, for example), and that Easter drama actually developed more slowly in the eleventh and twelfth centuries than did the burgeoning drama written for other occasions in the liturgical year. Rosemary Woolf, in her recent *The English Mystery Plays*, has offered substantial corroborating evidence that the use of the vernacular was not a "secularizing" process looking forward to the Corpus Christi cycles, but a literary technique used to enrich the dramatic effect of particular scenes.[4]

Perhaps the most significant re-evaluation of the evolutionary hypothesis has concerned itself with the relationship between church drama of the twelfth through fourteenth centuries and the cycle drama of the late fourteenth to sixteenth centuries. Did Corpus Christi drama evolve from church drama? The case once seemed a simple one. After all, both dramas treat of the divine history of the world, one chiefly in Latin and one in the English vernacular. Church drama furnished complex plays about Christmas and Easter, thus embracing the major events in the life of Christ. Nonetheless, as V. A. Kolve has shown in his *The Play Called Corpus Christi*, textual links between church drama and the Corpus Christi cycles are virtually nonexistent.[5] Church drama

---

3. O. B. Hardison, Jr., *Christian Rite and Christian Drama in the Middle Ages* (Baltimore, 1965), Essay I.
4. Rosemary Woolf, *The English Mystery Plays* (Berkeley and Los Angeles, 1972), pp. 42 ff.
5. V. A. Kolve, *The Play Called Corpus Christi* (London, 1966), pp. 39 ff. See also Woolf, *English Mystery Plays*, pp. 3 ff., and Grace Frank, *The Medieval French Drama* (Oxford, 1954), p. 67.

provided no instances of plays about Noah, Abraham and Isaac, Moses and Pharaoh, Christ's baptism, his temptation in the wilderness, the episode of the woman taken in adultery, and still others. Although Christmas and Easter plays were available in Latin church drama, even for these subjects we find no Corpus Christi text based on a translation from Latin drama. One reason for this striking discontinuity in medieval drama, as Kolve demonstrates, is that medieval monastic communities had only a few church plays each, perhaps two or three on the average; many church plays were in existence but they were scattered all over Europe. They simply were not anthologized with a view to producing a cycle. Cycle drama found an important precedent, to be sure, in the very fact that Latin church drama had dramatized large portions of the divine history of the world. Other than that, however, Corpus Christi drama began anew with its texts, relying on such nondramatic sources as Mirk's Festial or the *Cursor Mundi* or the so-called New Testament Apocrypha rather than on Latin dramatic texts.

Moreover, a similar period of discontinuity appears to be observable only a short time later, toward the end of the Middle Ages. Although morality drama may well have felt during its infancy the influence of the Corpus Christi cycles, especially in matters of staging, the morality play as a genre was not an evolutionary successor to the cycles. It seems to have derived much of its thematic content and approach to characterization from medieval sermons. As an acting tradition, the morality play soon parted company from cyclical and panoramic methods of production (whether on pageant wagons or in the round) in favour of itinerant performances on a highly mobile stage. In subject matter, the morality play proved capable of adapting itself to the constantly shifting political and religious obsessions of Reformation England, whereas the Corpus Christi cycles remained attuned to an essentially different and unchanging view of historical time.

We can observe, then, two major discontinuities in medieval drama, as seen from the point of view of texts, sources, themes and staging. My purpose here is to discuss parallel discontinuities in acting traditions. By "traditions" I mean not only acting styles, but also professional matters of organization and employment. Who are these actors? What are their social backgrounds, their previous or current means of livelihood? Are they professionals or amateurs?

Do they employ boys and women? To what extent do shifts in these matters of organization affect other discontinuities in staging and theme?

Glynne Wickham's provocative study of *Early English Stages* provides a useful point of departure, especially for a consideration of the first alleged major discontinuity between church drama and the Corpus Christi cycles.[6] Although Wickham is one of those who have most eloquently defended medieval drama against the denigrating tendencies of nineteenth-century Protestant Whig-Liberalism, he has gone too far in the opposite direction and has ironically produced his own version of an almost perfect continuity between acting traditions of the church drama and of the cycles. All medieval religious drama, in Wickham's view, was essentially under the control of the church. Cycle drama was not banished from the churchyard because it was too "secular"; rather, cycle drama was produced by craft guilds in conjunction with the church. This view of cycle drama as having flourished under the church's blessing is now a generally accepted conclusion, but Wickham goes about fortifying it with some remarkable speculations. Surely, he proposes, the process by which clerical actors of church plays were replaced by secular actors of the cycles must have been cooperative and gradual. The process must have involved those intermediate types who were in the employment of the church but were not members of the regular clergy: first the secular clergy, then the friars, and lastly a multitude of unbeneficed priests, deacons and clerks. Wickham is so intent on his theory of gradual transition that he hypothesizes the existence of Latin cycle plays, especially during the thirteenth century, acted by clerics and then gradually translated into the vernacular. Although texts cannot be found to support this contention, Wickham is attracted to it by his theory of continuity in acting traditions. He says, for example: "There was no innate reason why the resident clergy of a cathedral city could not cast the large cyclic plays thus brought into existence: nor any for laymen to tackle vernacular versions of them. Some external catalysis alone could fuse the two."[7]

The arguments against this hypothesis are in fact considerable.

6. Glynne Wickham, *Early English Stages, 1300 to 1660*, Vol. I, 1300–1576 (London and New York, 1966), pp. 122 ff.
7. Ibid., p. 149.

First, as we have seen, the cycle plays are markedly different in their contents from any Latin church plays that have come down to us. Even when cycle plays treat of subjects covered by church plays, the cycles invariably go to other sources. Next, the Latin plays were not gathered together into cycles. Proto-cyclic experiments at Riga in 1204 and at Cividale in 1298 and 1303, along with the twelfth-century Anglo-Norman *Adam*, do indicate that various attempts were made at cyclical production, but none of these has any direct connection with the cycles of the fourteenth and fifteenth centuries. In fact, as Rosemary Woolf has convincingly shown, church drama did not make significant advances in form during the thirteenth and early fourteenth centuries.[8] After the great innovative expansions of the twelfth-century renaissance, as represented in the work of Hilarius, the Beauvais *Daniel*, and the plays of the Carmina Burana manuscript from the Bavarian monastery of Benediktbeuern, we find little that is startlingly original until the advent of the Corpus Christi cycles.

One undoubted reason for this stasis was the problem of clerical acting. Even though the church had sponsored the beginnings of a liturgical drama and had seen that drama flower into the rich productions of the twelfth-century renaissance, some church members were distinctly uneasy at the prospect of clerical acting – especially in public and out of doors. The play of *Adam*, staged evidently outside a church on an elaborate multi-level stage, probably represents the kind of play of which conservative spokesmen like Gerhoh of Reichersberg, Herrad of Landsberg, William of Waddington, and Robert Mannyng of Brunne were most fearful. Despite some clerical attempts at acting during the thirteenth century, then, the situation remained stymied for well over a century until the craft guilds of the fourteenth century were able to propound their strikingly new solution of non-clerical actors in religious plays.

In order to understand more fully the process by which the dilemma developed, we need to trace as best we can the history of clerical acting from the tenth century onward. In the earlier tropes and dramatic ceremonials of the tenth century, the participants were of course clerics. They took part in a dramatization of ritual that remained for some time both dramatic and liturgical;

8. Woolf, *English Mystery Plays*, pp. 77, 83–84.

in fact, we are faced with a difficulty in knowing when to call the clerical participants "actors." At first the dramatic ceremonials were performed entirely by members of monastic communities, often without any congregation present. Although secular clergy in cathedrals may also have performed early dramatic ceremonies, no documents exist to prove that they in fact did so. Virtually all of our early texts are Benedictine. Some of the earliest tenth-century *Quem quaeritis* texts, such as the simplest text of all from St. Gall (c. 950), may have been sung antiphonally by the choir as they approached the altar on Easter Sunday, without any assignment of individual roles. The more detailed text from the *Regularis Concordia* manuscript (965–975), for the Benedictine use in England, does assign roles to individual members of the choir for the three Marys and the angel at the tomb, and yet the concept of "acting" in this production is not fully developed. Clearly, the Marys are presented not by boy singers but by regular brethren of the monastic choir. Although they modulate their voices, carry thuribles to represent spices, and enter hesitantly as though looking for something, their actions are highly formalized. They chant their Latin lines derived from the Easter liturgy, and wear "costumes" (if the term is applicable) that have been easily fashioned out of the ecclesiastical garments worn by other members of the choir. In short, despite innovative mimetic effects, the brethren are still clerics participating in a religious ceremonial occasion attached to the liturgy of matins or of Easter mass. No congregation is present or necessary.

Several external factors point to the semantic difficulty of regarding the early *Quem quaeritis* dramatic ceremonials as plays, and their performers as actors. Virtually all tenth- and eleventh-century texts have been preserved in breviaries, ordinals and service books of this sort rather than in special collections devoted to plays or to other non-liturgical texts. Only when we come to manuscripts such as the Fleury playbook or the Benediktbeuern Carmina Burana, in the twelfth or early thirteenth centuries, do we find textual evidence that the scribes regarded their materials as no longer belonging to the official liturgy of the church. A similar phenomenon can be observed in the handling of stage directions and speech prefixes (to use modern terms in an anachronistic context). Clearly the stage directions of the early dramatic ceremonials are rubrics, analogous to those of a breviary or missal specifying how the priest officiating at a religious office is to move his hands or turn his body. The names of the speakers are fre-frequently imbedded in these rubrics, or are omitted when the speaker's identity is sufficiently implied, so that a modern editor cannot supply from the original text a simple speech prefix. When we come to the twelfth-century Anglo-Norman *Adam*, on the other hand, we find long portions of the manuscript with real speech prefixes for "Adam," "Eve" or "Devil." The twelfth-century Anglo-Norman *Seinte Resureccion* is even more consistent in this regard than *Adam*, and can in fact be edited from the original in con-formity with our modern practice of providing the beginning of every speech with the speaker's name.

These external considerations have interesting implications re-garding the status of "actors" in these early forms of church drama during the tenth and eleventh centuries. Because the concept of the actor emerges only slowly, and cannot be looked upon as fully developed until the twelfth-century flowering of a truly literary drama at centres of learning like Beauvais, Fleury and Benedikt-beuern, we should be cautious of asserting any rapid development in the use of dramatic methods (such as the use of boy actors) that we associate with drama of the later Middle Ages or even of the Renaissance. When, for example, Fletcher Collins claims in *The Production of Medieval Church Music-Drama* that the im-portance of the three Marys in early church drama "speaks well for the talent of the boy actor,"[9] we need to ask whether the Marys were in fact consistently performed by boys in church plays per-formed at Easter. What is the evidence for boy acting in church drama prior to the era of the Corpus Christi cycles?

Evidence from the rubrics of the plays themselves argues against the extensive use of boy singers. The rubrics of the *Regularis Concordia* Visit to the Sepulchre speak of "four brethren" who are to vest themselves as the angel and the three Marys. In the text doubtfully ascribed to Aquileia, Italy (c. eleventh century), "two brethren" represent the holy women. The presence of a congrega-tion at this ceremonial does not appear to require the use of a more verisimilar effect. In the *Visitatio Sepulchri* from St. Lambrecht, from the same period, a deacon represents the angel at the tomb. Although students take part in the procession, together with their

9. Fletcher Collins, Jr., *The Production of Medieval Church Music-Drama* (Charlottesville, Va., 1972), p. 16.

schoolmaster, the performers of the *Visitatio* itself are all senior members of the choir. The famous Fleury playbook, a sophisticated literary work from the later twelfth century, assigns the parts of the three Marys to "three brethren." A fifteenth-century manuscript from Rouen, embodying a tradition of that cathedral from the thirteenth through fifteenth centuries, assigns the roles of the Marys to three deacons.[10] Grace Frank notes that the following terms are used to refer to the three Marys and the angels in the *Visitatio* throughout the Middle Ages: *cantores, custodes chori, fratres, pueri, capellani, diacones, sacerdotes, presbiteri,* and *scholares*.[11] Most of these terms apply not only to adult males but to the senior clergy. (The occasional mention of *pueri* or *scholares* refers usually to the angels at the tomb rather than to the three Marys.) Thus the tradition of using adult male voices in the Visit to the Sepulchre lived long; Collins is surely wrong in assuming the customary use of boy singers. Generally, too, the senior clergy were employed for major roles not only in the Visit to the Sepulchre but in other church drama as well. At Rouen, for example, the three Magi were represented by "tres clerici de maiori sede,"[12] and in another text the apostles were portrayed by "antiquiores et honorabiliores canonici."[13] The tradition of male singing seems even to have influenced the visual arts; in an illustration from an eleventh-century manuscript from Beaucaire and Modena, the three Marys who are visiting the spice merchant are clearly men.[14]

A Benedictine manuscript of the fourteenth and fifteenth centuries from a convent at Barking, England, reveals that women were used to play the parts of the three Marys.[15] A decorum of this sort in regard to sex was obviously practical in a convent, where there were also enough priests on hand to undertake male

10. Young, *Drama of the Medieval Church*, I, 370–371. Other *Quem quaeritis* texts cited in this paragraph are also to be found in Young, Vol. I.
11. Frank, *Medieval French Drama*, p. 69.
12. Young, *Drama of the Medieval Church*, II, 436.
13. O. Schüttpelz, *Der Wettlauf der Apostel und die Erscheinungen des Peregrinispiels im geistlichen Spiel des Mittelalters* (Breslau, 1930), p. 25; cited in Frank, *Medieval French Drama*, p. 69.
14. G. Cohen, "The Influence of the Mysteries on Art in the Middle Ages," *Gazette des beaux-arts*, 6th series, XXIV (1943), 329–330; cited in Woolf, *English Mystery Plays*, p. 96.
15. Woolf, *English Mystery Plays*, p. 20.

roles. The practice was confined to convents, however, as far as is known.

The first seemingly clear use of choir boys in church drama is in the Slaughter of the Innocents from the Fleury playbook. Presumably the Innocents themselves are boys, or postulants for admission to the monastery.[16] They are dressed in white stoles, and rejoicingly enter the monastery church in procession behind the figure of the lamb bearing the cross of Christ. Significantly, however, the boys' role is almost entirely limited to that of choral singing. They enter chanting "O how glorious is the kingdom," an antiphon for vespers on the Vigil of All Saints, and subsequently chant other appropriate antiphons and hymns. They sing only one line in the entire drama that is not a regular liturgical composition of this sort. The Fleury play also contains a substantial role for the lamenting mother Rachel, but we cannot assume with any certainty that a boy took this part; the weight of evidence tends in fact to support the contrary conclusion that the part may have been sung by an adult male.

The pattern found in the Fleury Innocents play suggests by analogy that choirs of boys were used elsewhere in church drama, to represent the angels announcing Christ's nativity to the shepherds and for similar choric effects. In the Benediktbeuern Passion Play (late twelfth century), "Hebrew boys" chant "Hosanna in the highest" during Christ's entry into Jerusalem. In addition, we find a Boy Bishop present in the Benediktbeuern Christmas play, though his participation is limited to one speech in contrast to the demanding roles assigned St. Augustine, Archisynagogus and other prominent characters. An unusually substantial role, seemingly for a boy chorister, is to be found in the twelfth-century Fleury St. Nicholas play about Adeodatus, son of Getron, who is abducted from his parents by King Marmorinus and ultimately restored by St. Nicholas. Despite Adeodatus' centrality to the plot, however, his speeches are only five in number and do not attempt the passionate utterance found, for example, in the lament of his mother.

This internal evidence concerning boy actors does not, in any case, give support to a hypothesis that boys must have been used extensively for solo women's parts, as, for example, in the demand-

16. Arnold Williams, *The Drama of Medieval England* (Michigan State University Press, 1961), p. 25.

ing role of Eve in the Anglo-Norman *Adam*. In point of fact, we simply do not know how that play was cast. The general assumption has been that it was clerically performed, but even that assumption is based on the broader supposition that twelfth-century church plays never employed non-clerical actors, rather than on any evidence in the play itself. We can assume with greater confidence that the Benediktbeuern Passion play was performed by clerics, but we do not know if the part of Mary Magdalene was sung by a boy chorister or by an adult male. Generally, church drama contains relatively few demanding roles for women; such plays from Fleury as the Pilgrim play or the Conversion of St. Paul have all-male casts. In other cases, occasional women's roles could have been sung by men. If men sang the parts of the three Marys throughout the Middle Ages, they might also have undertaken such roles as the Virgin Mary in the Passion play or Mary Magdalene and her sister in the Raising of Lazarus.

Church drama seems to have been slow to move in the direction of fitting women or boy singers to women's parts, just as it was slow to adopt other verisimilar effects. After all, casting must have begun as a musically-directed function rather than as a theatrically-directed function. Voices were fitted from the choir in terms of their experience and musical ability. Repeatedly the rubrics of the plays direct the singer to sing "in a moderate or very dignified voice" (Fleury *Visitatio Sepulchri*), or in a similar manner. Boys took their places as neophytes and as upper voices in the choir, usually singing in unison. Such traditions, once established, proved remarkably persistent. Clerical renditions of the Visit to the Sepulchre continued on well into the Renaissance much as they had been performed in the tenth and eleventh centuries.

These considerations about "actors" as singers in a liturgically oriented church drama may cast some light on the problem of discontinuity between church drama and the cycles. We can perhaps understand better why church conservatives such as Gerhoh disapproved of clerical acting in public, when we see that church drama had circumscribed its histrionic range to deliberately narrow limits. Despite the unequalled splendour of a drama like the Beauvais *Daniel* or the Benediktbeuern Christmas play, we find in clerical acting tradition no precedent for Noah's wife or the Alewife of the Chester Harrowing of Hell. Among adult male roles we find no precedent for the comic insolence of Christ's torturers or Mak the sheep stealer. Church drama remained a chanted musical drama, highly stylized and formal. The actors were, by training and tradition, unsuited for the kind of theatre we find in the cycles. To be sure, the case for discontinuity must not be overstated. In the Anglo-Norman *Adam*, presumably acted by clerics, devils make forays across the platea and among the spectators. Festive traditions of misrule at Christmas, especially among the minor clergy, yield precedents for clerical horseplay and lampooning. Chaucer reminds us that the part of "Herodes upon a skaffold hye" was played by Absalom, a parish clerk.[17] The Cividale protocycle of 1303 was performed "by the clergy, or by the lay chapter" – a phrase that may suggest the participation of the laity.[18] Glynne Wickham is not wrong in supposing that the minor clergy were involved in periodic attempts to enlarge the scope of church drama and render it more amenable to popular taste. He does appear to be wrong, however, in assuming that a coherent and extensive Latin cyclical drama emerged from such fitful undertakings, and that such a Latin cyclical drama needed only to be translated into English in order to produce the Corpus Christi cycles. Everything we know about the acting of church drama confirms our impression that it occupied a strikingly different world from that of cyclical drama, and that efforts at bridging the gap were doomed to be sporadic. What cyclical drama needed was a new source of manpower for the acting of outdoor plays.

A key fact about casting in the cycles is that it follows no single pattern. One community or guild might evolve different solutions from those of another community or guild, and the process might also change at any given community over a period of time. The same was true of staging: in some places or at various times the plays were performed processionally on pageant wagons, whereas at other places or times the plays were performed in one place. These variable factors of casting and staging are, as we shall see, interrelated. The Corpus Christi cycles were experimental in method, and this very fact of experiment and variety argues against a continuous process of evolution from church drama.

Women's parts may have been assigned more frequently to boys in the cycles than in church drama, although we certainly

17. Chaucer, "The Miller's Tale," ll. 3312 and 3384, in *The Works of Geoffrey Chaucer*, ed. F. N. Robinson, 2nd ed. (Boston, 1957).
18. Williams, *Drama of Medieval England*, p. 50.

David Bevington

cannot assume that the practice was invariable. For one thing, guild records are not always clear about the ages of actors performing women's roles: the Coventry accounts for the Smith's Company in 1495 record a payment to "Ryngold's man Thomas thatt playtt Pylatts wyff," but do not indicate whether Thomas was a boy apprentice or a young man. Payment was also made three years later to "Pylatts wyffe for his wages," without indicating if the actor was this same Thomas.[19] For another thing, roles in the cycles do not always demand the talents of a young boy actor even where we would normally expect to find juvenile casting. Although the well-known Brome Abraham and Isaac seems to conceive of Isaac as a child, the Towneley and York versions of this pageant do not, and medieval theological interpretation often supports the view that Isaac need not be considered especially young.[20] On the other hand, we do find some clear indications that small children were used in production. Two sixteenth-century records of payment at Coventry are for child actors, one "to the woman for her chyld" (Weaver's Pageant, 1551) and the other "to the letell chylde" (Weaver's, 1553).[21] In France, 1424, we find an entire mystère of the Old and New Testaments put on by "les enfens de Paris" in tableau vivant.[22] Conceivably, too, women were employed as actors. At Chester, the "wyfus of ye town" were responsible at one time for a pageant on the Assumption of the Virgin. Whether the women actually performed the roles or merely sponsored the production cannot be said with certainty, but a play with such major women's roles would be appropriate to the wives. Women were paid for appearing in a London Lord Mayor's show in 1523, and a few other isolated instances of female acting are on record.[23] Generally, then, female roles in the cycle plays were handled in a variety of ways, with boy actors as one common possibility.

A significant new development in the casting of Corpus Christi

19. Hardin Craig, ed., *Two Coventry Corpus Christi Plays*, 2nd ed. (Oxford, 1957), p. 87.
20. Williams, *Drama of Medieval England*, p. 68.
21. Craig, *Coventry Plays*, p. 106.
22. *Journal d'un bourgeois de Paris, 1405–1449*, ed. A. Tuetey (Paris, 1881), p. 200; cited in Woolf, *English Mystery Plays*, p. 97.
23. Salter, *Medieval Drama at Chester*, p. 48; Wickham, *Early English Stages*, I, 271; and Allardyce Nicoll, *Masks, Mimes, and Miracles* (London, 1931), p. 192.

drama was the use not only of lay actors but of professional actors. Some of the many payments made to actors in guild and municipal records were for amateur performance by local guild members, of course. Amateur acting must have been common in the early years of the Corpus Christi plays, especially if (as Alan Nelson has recently argued) the plays grew out of the Corpus Christi procession.[24] The guilds, after all, were obliged to accompany the Host in the Corpus Christi procession, with banners, torches and often with tableau vivant displays on pageant wagons. If these festive displays in the procession gave birth to processional plays, the guilds may well have learned from their participation in the procession itself to supply amateur players for dramatic performances. As the plays grew more elaborate, however, the performance of those plays tended to become separate from the Corpus Christi procession and to be acted on some occasions in a fixed place. Portions of the N Town Cycle were certainly acted in a single location, and other cycles may also have adopted such a method of production.

The development of fixed-location staging undoubtedly encouraged professionalism in acting. Performance of this sort employed one actor for a major role throughout a sequence rather than providing a new actor for each individual segment. If a separate cast was employed for each individual pageant wagon at York, for example, twenty-seven Christs must have been required for a complete performance. If the Towneley plays at Wakefield were acted on pageant wagons, a total cast of 243 actors would have been required. Such inefficiencies must have posed enormous problems, especially in a small town like Wakefield, and in fact we cannot be at all sure that the Towneley cycle was acted processionally by individual guilds; only a very few pageants (three) in the manuscript are assigned to guilds, and these assignments are in a sixteenth-century script. York, on the other hand, was a fairly large town with a sizeable number of powerful guilds. The York text with its unusually short segments of action, especially in the Old Testament sequence, may well represent an amateur and guild

---

24. Alan Nelson, *The English Corpus Christi Play: Processional Pageants and Cycle Drama* (Chicago, 1974). Chambers, *Mediaeval Stage*, II, 133 ff., argues that the already-existing plays were adapted to the Corpus Christi procession, but supports the view that the plays were profoundly influenced by conditions of performance in the procession.

tendency to divide the action among many players with short roles rather than among relatively few players with long roles (although even at York many of the actors may have come to be professionals). Performance at a fixed place offered considerable efficiency in the handling of major continuing roles, but it also meant a giving up of individual control over individual parts of the cycle and a consequent centralizing and professionalizing of the production. Assignments of continuing major roles to actors required that those actors be highly skilled and well paid. Records of payment at Lincoln, for example, suggest a significant distinction between guild actors assigned minor and amateur roles, and professional actors assigned major roles. The Cordwainers at Lincoln evidently provided three men as shepherds for their Nativity sequence, but paid "the plaiers" for more substantial parts.[25] Presumably the roles of Joseph and Mary were not supplied by the guild because they were continuing characters through a large portion of the cycle. The actors of these parts were paid by the religious guild in charge of the overall cycle rather than by an individual craft guild.

The extent of professionalism in the acting of late medieval drama has probably been underestimated, both in the cycles and in pageant-like displays such as royal entries and Lord Mayor's shows.[26] Professional entertainers were, after all, plentifully available even if the church had long frowned on their activities. They tended to represent themselves as minstrels and troubadours rather than as players, but texts such as the *Interludium de Clerico et Puella* (fourteenth century) attest to a tradition of secular play-acting that had never entirely disappeared.[27] These professional entertainers seem to have profited from the church's solution to its problem of clerical acting in outdoor plays, which was, as we have seen, to allow lay actors to perform vernacular religious plays under the aegis of combined ecclesiastical and civic control. This allowance of lay acting, though extended perhaps at first to

25. Kenneth Cameron and Stanley J. Kahrl, "Staging the N-Town Cycle," *Theatre Notebook*, XXI (Spring, 1967), 122–138.
26. David Bergeron, "Actors in English Civic Pageants," *Renaissance Papers 1972* (1973), pp. 17–28, has come to similar conclusions about Lord Mayor's shows in the later Renaissance. See also Nicoll, *Masks, Mimes, and Miracles*, pp. 192–194.
27. See, for example, R. G. Thomas, ed., *Ten Miracle Plays* (Evanston, 1966), p. 8.

amateur members of craft guilds, seems also to have encompassed the professionals and part-time professionals who became more and more involved in the cycles as these dramas grew more and more elaborate and costly in production. Professional players were now acting under church sponsorship. Yet this development seems to have provoked no outcry from the church, since the plays were after all religious plays under ecclesiastical control. The only complaints against drama during the fourteenth and fifteenth centuries came from Wycliffe and his Lollards, precursors of sixteenth-century reform objections to idolatry in dramatic art.

The thrust of professionalism can be seen in the phenomenon of touring. The N Town cycle is particularly interesting in this regard, for it was evidently designed to be performed in a series of towns and was provided with banns for advance publicity in each locale. The banns end with an announcement that performance will take place in "N Town," with the actual name of the town to be supplied by the speaker in each individual case. This enormous cycle production could not have been taken easily or far on tour, we must suppose, but the very attempt reinforces our impression of a professional cast searching out audiences and gate receipts. The early fifteenth-century morality play, *The Castle of Perseverance*, was evidently toured in a similar fashion, since its famous staging design calls for a surrounding moat or a fence depending on local circumstances.

With professional touring we are on the verge of the second major discontinuity in acting traditions during the Middle Ages, that from the Corpus Christi drama to the itinerant morality play. I call this a "discontinuity" despite the evidence that professionals acted in the cycles as well as in the morality; after all, some similar overlap must also have occurred in the earlier transition from church drama to Corpus Christi drama. Even allowing for these overlaps, the break with the past is in both cases decisive. Clerical actors gave way to the secular actors of a great civic drama, both amateur and professional; and civic drama soon found itself competing with a professional theatre of small itinerant troupes specializing in the morality play and all its mutant forms. Corpus Christi drama and morality drama coexisted for a long period of time in the fifteenth and sixteenth centuries, and in fact morality drama actually began (as we can see in *The Castle of Persever-ance*) in a staging tradition much like that of the cycles. Nevertheless, the itinerant troupes enjoyed an enormous advantage in their ability to travel easily and to act in every kind of arena from village green to town hall to nobleman's banqueting hall. The morality play proved equally flexible in doctrinal content and in its protean ability to reflect the issues of contemporary English life. Without the professionalization of England's acting corps, Tudor drama would have been far less able to develop those qualities of a truly popular theatre which were inherited by Shakespeare, Marlowe and other dramatists of the late sixteenth century.

"To find the players and all that longeth therto": Notes on the Production of Medieval Drama in Coventry

R. W. INGRAM

Although I shall touch generally on the Coventry Corpus Christi Play, I intend to concentrate on the dramatic productions of the Cappers' Company, especially their pageant-play of *The Resurrection, The Harrowing of Hell*, and *The Meeting with the Maries*. The play was lost sometime after 1597 (see 1597 inventory below) but the Cappers' accounts contain much interesting if often puzzling information about it. My notes, therefore, will ask rather than answer questions and will deal with the identity of Robert Crow, Capper, playwright, actor and property-man; the number of performances the pageant received; the revisions it underwent; some Capper actors; and, finally, stage properties, costumes and the stage itself. These discussions are prefaced by a comment on the nature of the Cappers' accounts and the overall cost of pageant production in the sixteenth century.

The Cappers' Account Book

The Company and Fellowship of Cappers and Feltmakers, happily, still exists, and by their kind permission I quote freely from their earliest surviving account book which begins in 1494. There is a gap in these accounts from 1556 to 1571. The years to 1561 are inexplicably blank but those from 1562 to 1571 were covered in a smaller account book (destroyed in 1879) from which Sharp and

Halliwell-Phillipps made valuable extracts. None the less the coverage for the missing years is scanty.[1]

The extant accounts are rich in information about play production but vary considerably in scope and content. Occasionally no details of pageant expenses are given, merely the total cost for the year (as in 1535, 1536, 1538 and 1541). This is frustrating for the dramatic historian. A detailed account must have existed from which the sum total was computed. Possibly it was entered elsewhere; the Weavers, for instance, occasionally listed some of their pageant costs in their Rentgatherers' Book rather than in the main account book: possibly the detailed accounts existed on separate sheets or in bills that were once in the Company's safe-box. Whether they are lengthy or tantalizingly brief, the pageant accounts present problems of interpretation. They are often shorthand reminders rather than full clear records. "The mattr of the castell at emaus" in 1553 (f. 82b) needed no further explanation at that time; the costly "suettelts" and lavish entertainments enjoyed at Candlemas, 1525, were doubtless amply vivid in the memories of all, but we can only guess what the details were (f. 36a).

The accounts are not rigorously organized. Errors in addition are not uncommon, for Tudor accountants are as fallible as today's computers. Headings are sometimes guides rather than absolute rules: in 1543, "expensys & payments abowt the pageant and the pleyars" wander into items concerning the Midsummer Night's

---

1. Special thanks are due to Lord Iliffe, Master of the Cappers' Company, and Mr. Julian Hoare, Clerk to the Company, whose generosity and aid went far beyond the granting of permission to use the Account Book. Cappers' references are to this book save for the missing years where I rely upon T. Sharp, *A Dissertation on the Pageants or Dramatic Mysteries Anciently Performed at Coventry* (Coventry, 1825), e.g. S49; J. O. Halliwell-Phillipps, *Outlines of the Life of Shakespeare*, 2 vols. (7th ed., Brighton, 1887), e.g. H-P *Outlines* II, 289, and extracts from the latter's 56 volumes of scrapbooks in the Folger Library, e.g. H-P Wb 177, p. 56. References to other guild records are to material in the City Record Office at Coventry, where the aid over the years of the City Archivist, A. A. Dibben (and his predecessor Miss D. A. Leech) and D. J. H. Smith I gratefully acknowledge. I am also grateful to the Broadweavers' and Clothiers' Company for permission to use their Account Book and their Rentgatherers' Book (they begin in 1523 and 1521). The Drapers' Account Book, beginning in 1534, exists only in a mid-nineteenth-century transcript by T. Daffern and I am grateful to the City of Coventry Council for permission to study it (e.g. D 39).

processions. The Clerk catches himself in the slip so he pauses, sums up the money so far listed against pageant expenses, including the two errant items, writes his next subheading, "more expensys on mydsomer night," and carries on with what he had inadvertently begun (f. 59b). In 1550, the "expensys of the pageande" close with 7d. "pd for hengys and nales for the plasterars house" (77b). At this period the plasterer was renting his house from the Cappers for 14s. a year: could it be that his was also the pageant-house where the wagon and scaffolds were stored? Almost certainly not, for in 1547 John Cowper not only put in a day repairing the "plasterars howse" but was also paid for other work on the pageant-house door (f. 69b). But for the chance of those repairs the supposition would not have been an idle one: the Drapers rented both their old pageant-house and their new one; in addition they rented the garden of the latter as well (1541 f. 19a, 1562 f. 51a).[2]

The facts to be found in the Cappers' Accounts are rich and various but before turning to examine some of them more closely it is well to bear in mind the pleasant if tantalizingly idiosyncratic nature of the whole record.

The Financing of the Cappers' Play

Medieval Coventry, it was said, was built on the woolsack – its wealth and national importance was founded on the cloth trade. Throughout the vicissitudes of the cloth trade, while other crafts connected with it were declining during the first part of the sixteenth century, the Cappers were flourishing. Capping was an ancient trade in the city but little is known of it until April 1496, when it was so well-founded that "the Maistirs & ffeliship" (a body of twenty-four men, among them two future mayors) "shewed & brought . . . the boke of their ordenaunces" for confirmation before the Leet. Their growing prosperity was such that in a 1522 survey listing 635 people representing 90 different trades and occupations, the three leading occupations were Cappers 83, Weavers 41 and Shearman 38. Also among the top twelve, and of interest because of the trades' associations with the Corpus Christi Plays, were

2. It appears that Coventry was not one of those corporations that made an income from the leasing of pageant-houses (see G. Wickham, *Early English Stages* I [London and New York, 1959], p. 296).

Drapers 28 (6th), Dyers 28 (6th), Mercers 26 (9th), Tailors 21 (10th), Tanners 15 (11th), and Smiths 14 (12th).[3]

In 1496 the Cappers did not have a pageant but the year before, perhaps as an indication of their civic responsibility, had told the Leet that "of theire goode will they were agreeable to paye" 6s. 8d yearly towards the expenses of the Girdlers' pageant (Leet 565). An order of Leet in October 1529 releases the Walkers from contributing to the Girdlers' pageant and raises the Cappers' contribution to 13s. 4d. (Leet 699). There are no Cappers' Accounts for 1530 but in September of that year a further order of Leet released them from the 6s. 8d. due to the Girdlers "for certeyn consideracions" not specified (Leet 701–702). This order presumably countermanded that of the previous year. By this time the Cappers, a powerful group of nearly fifty brethren, wanted not only their own pageant but their own chapel in the great parish church of St. Michael. In October 1531 they were associated with the Cardmakers and Saddlers, a guild fallen on hard times and "beyng now but a fewe persones in nomber," as partners "in the gouernance, reparyng, & meynteynyng, as well of & in the seid Chappell, named Seynt Thomas Chappell, & of the ornamentes and lightes of the same, As of & in the seid pagyaunt And pagiaunt house with the Implementes, appurtenaunces, pleaers, reherces, & pleyng geire accustumed, belongyng & necessarie to & for the same, after suche maner or better as it hathe been used & accustumed before tyme" (Leet 708–709). On April 24, 1537, the Leet confirmed what had already happened, that the Cardmakers had "latelie surrendered & given upp by wrytyng" all rights to the chapel and pageant to the Cappers. As can be seen, the Cappers had been entering the expenses of the pageant in their own accounts since 1534.

As a reminder of the number of people who chiefly supported the Cappers' production of their play the following figures record the craft members paying quarterage dues at five-yearly intervals throughout the sixteenth century: 1500 – 23; 1505 – 16; 1510 – 27; 1515 – 32; 1520 – 42; 1525 – 52; 1530 – 45; 1535 – 59; 1540 – 57; 1545 – 54; 1550 – 65; 1555 – 73; 1556–1571 – no records; 1572 – 49;

3. The fuller survey, upon which this paragraph is based, is in Joan C. Lancaster, "Crafts and Industries" in *Victoria County History of Warwick*, VIII (1969), pp. 155–160. The Leet references are to *The Coventry Leet Book*, ed. M. D. Harris, EETS o.s. 135 (1907–1913).

1575 – 60; 1579 – 60; 1584 – 51 (the City and the guilds combined to put on a new religious play called *The Destruction of Jerusalem*); 1591 – 36 (City and guilds again combined in either a repeat of *Jerusalem* or, possibly, some other dramatic show). In addition to these are the apprentices whose number ranges from 2 to 15 in a year, and the journeymen. Only in the accounts for 1548 are the latter listed and then they number 47. Thus, in 1548, the Company mustered at least 118 members, 59 brethren, 47 journeymen and 12 new apprentices (an unknown number of apprentices from earlier years – at least 5 – must also be allowed for). The income of the Company derived from membership payments (6d. at least by each brother at each of the two quarterages), apprenticeship fees, occasional journeymen's collections such as that of 1548 (it brought in 15s. 8d.), fines, rents of properties plus charges for chapel services. There were also such gatherings as that for the minstrel which may have been more regular than the two mentions of it suggest, and the journeymen's yearly fees contributed towards the pageant that are called for by the Company rules and expected by the city but rarely recorded. The yearly expenses were the pageant, processions at Midsummer, St. Peter's Eve, Corpus Christi and sundry celebrations of a variety of special civic and holy days and, of course, the Guild's own dinners.[4] Although the Cappers' receipts over the fifty years from 1534 varied between a little over £4 to something over £17, their expenses usually kept pace with the fluctuations, so that in nearly every year the Company's treasury was augmented.

Sharp, writing of the Cappers, remarked that "the annual charge for playing the Pageant was about 35s. until 1550, afterwards 45s. to 50s" (536). As little is known of the yearly costs of producing a pageant I have extracted the following list. For each year, where known, between 1534 and 1591 I give first the total expenses and then, where possible, an indication of how much was spent on repairs (to the pageant-wagon, scaffolds, pageant-house, costumes, properties, etc.). The remaining amount covers the regular expenses of rehearsals, actors' wages, food and drink for the Master and his friends at the overseeing of the rehearsals, for the actors

---

4. An excellent treatment of these celebrations will be found in C. Phythian-Adams, "Ceremony and the citizen: The communal year at Coventry 1450–1550," in P. Clark and P. Slack, eds., *Crisis and Order in English Towns 1500–1700* (1972), pp. 57–85.

and for the drivers, and such recurring items as gloves, points, rushes, etc.

1534: 61s. 7½d.	: 31s. 5½d.	Cappers take over pageant
1535: 34s. 5d.		
1536: 34s. 9d.		summary total only in accounts
1538: 30s. 8d.		
1539: 33s. 9½d.	: 1s. 1d.	hooks, nails, wright for day & half
1540: 38s. 1½d.	: 2s. 6½d.	Pilate's mall made for 1s. 10d.
1541: 35s. 4d.	: 1s.	summary totals only in accounts
1542: 33s. 8d.	: 1s. 2½d.	thread and nails
1543: 53s. 8d.	: 22s. 2½d.	much work on p-house and wagon: demon's head made 1s. 6d.
1544: 46s. 11d.	: 7s. 3d.	skaffolds; painting mall, rattell, spade, 2 crosses, hellmouth
1547: 34s. 0½d.	: 4s. 4½d.	Spirit of God's coat 2s. 8d.; 2 stars 1s., diadem 4d.
1548: 38s. 3d.	: 5s. 6d.	P-house, p-wheels.
1549: 42s. 6d.	: 6s. 8d.	Pilate's doublet 1s. 10d. plus 3s. 4d. drink at same time
1550: 50s. 7d.	: 10s. 11d.	Bishop's gowns 4s. 8d., mending demon's coat 3s., surplice 1s.
1551: 49s. 4d.	: 42s.	costs of "nwe payntyng the pageant": rehearsal costs but no performance costs
1552: 46s. 4d.	: 8s. 8d.	"castell of emaus" and new play book
1553: 61s. 4d.	: 13s. 5d.	p-wheels, Pilate's mall remade 2s. 1d., trestles 1s. 8d.
1554: 45s. 6d.	: 1s. 6d.	
1555: 55s. 11d.	: 9s. 5d.	4s. 9d. for cressetts

1556–1571 incomplete figures except for 1563 (H-P Wb 155, p. 31) and 1565 (S 49–50 corrected by H-P Wb 177, pp. 12–13)

1562:	: 5s. 6d.	mending demon's coat & making his head 5s.
1563: 44s. 10d.	: 2s. 4d.	"mendynge of the pagyand, xx^d," balls 8d.
1565: 89s. 11d.	: 23s.	wagon & wheels 12s. 2d., furring bishops' hoods 8s.
1566:	: 3s. 6d.	"prickynge the songes, xvj^d"
1567:	: 1s.	"assyden for Pilat head, ij^d"
1568:	: 7s. 9d.	songs 12d, making hellmouth new 1s. 9d.

1569:	: 7s.	wagon 5s. 8d.
1571:	: 1s. 11d.	mending costumes of demon and Maries
1572: 75s. 1d.		details not filled in on page left blank for purpose
1573: 50s. 5d.	: 13s. 8d.	timber and "axeltre" for wagon & skaffold
1574: 63s. 1d.	: 15s. 10d.	wheels: entertaining cardmakers 6s. 10d.
		26s. 8d. from cardmakers, walkers, skinners, joiners
1575: 3s. 0d.		One rehearsal then plague cancelled pageants
1576: 77s. 7d.	: 24s. 6d.	From Walkers 6s. Skinners 4s., Joiners 3s. 4d. (until 1579)
		wagon & costume repairs
1577: 60s. 3d.	: 9s. 3d.	wagon
1578: 65s. 11d.	: 11s. 2d.	
1579: 72s. 2d.	: 13s. 5d.	p-house and wagon
1584: 50s. 6d.	: 11s. 4d.	costumes, skaffold, play-book 5s.: apparently shared with Shearmen & Tailors
1591: 21s. 6d.	: 1s. 6d.	received from walkers 6s. 8d., Skinners 4s., Joiners 3s. 4d.

There is no mathematical formula that can translate these six-teenth-century prices into those of today, the more so as prices themselves changed greatly during the sixteenth century. The complete entry for 1564 in the Leet Book is not typical but is indicative of the capacity of prices startlingly to alter: "In the beginninge of this yere one Stryke of wheate was at Eighte Shil-linges and one Strike of rye at Sixe Shillinges, but in the ende of the same yere a strike of wheate was at fourtene pence And a strike of Rye at tenne pence" (Leet 819). Certainly the overall cost of producing the pageant rose for the Cappers. By and large the actors' wages remained stable but in other items the rise can be measured. The price of points rose steadily from 4d. in 1534, through 5d., 6d., 8d., 10d., to 12d. in 1579. Gloves for the first ten years vary between 1s. 4d. and 1s. 8d. the set (usually eighteen pair) but by 1579 they cost 4s. 6d. Even the rushes for the pageant wagon floor rise from 1d. to 4d. The leather balls which Pilate, in some unknown way, used up in large numbers each year, cost 5d. in 1544 for sixteen made out of two skins of leather; by the seventies the annual cost was 12d. Driving the pageant wagon earned Lewez 6d. in 1534. The drivers (the journeymen had to provide the eight, ten or twelve men to haul the wagon along) had 8d. to buy them drink for their labour. By 1540 the ten men receive 2d. each and 14d. to buy drink. Their rates rise to 3s. and 4s. and eventually level out (if that is the word) at 6s. 8d.

The Cappers were fond of drinking and dining and many of their business meetings include a handsome allowance for such entertainment. In 1549 they spent 1s. 10d. on a new doublet for Pilate but "spent at the crane att the pottyng owt" of it, 3s. 4d. (f. 74b). In the pageant drink was regularly supplied to the drivers and to the actors before, during and after the performances. In the seventies, however, perhaps in an effort towards economy, only Pilate, the four knights and the two bishops were allowed drink between the stages; in the last three years of production the two bishops were taken from this list. The Leet often had to fix the price of ale: in 1522 it was put at 18d. the cester, the cester being set at fourteen gallons. Seven years later it was 2s. the cester and the cester was reduced to thirteen gallons, and where ale was sold by the gallon or less the price was to be no more than 3d. a gallon. In 1565 pageant ale was costing the Cappers 4d. a gallon, a year later the Smiths were paying 6d. The worth of an ale standard, as it might be called, at a time when it was possibly safer as a drink than much water, may be measured by the fact that in 1520 the consumption of ale in Coventry was 12,118 gallons a week, a two pints daily for every man, woman and child in the city.[5]

Another measure is provided by wage rates fixed by order of Leet. In 1496 the Cappers included in their ordinances the setting of a journeyman's wage (for a twelve-hour day) at 12d. a week (with a fine of 6s. 8d. for any master who paid more) (Leet 574). In 1553 summer wages of master carpenters were fixed at 8d. a day, with 6d. a day for journeymen and satisfactory apprentices; master tilers and rough masons were to receive 7d. a day, and their labourers 5d.; daubers were to receive 6d. a day and their labourers 5d. Common labourers' rates were fixed at 5d. a day. During

5. G. G. Coulton's figures (based on Leet records) quoted in F. Smith, *Coventry: Six Hundred Years of Municipal Life* (1945), pp. 78–79.

winter (that is between November 1 and February 2) all received a penny or twopence less (Leet 806-7).[6]

The orders of Leet continually refer to matters of prices and wages and general financial and commercial ordering of the citizens' affairs. The majority of the orders referring to pageants have to do also with what financial aid various guilds should either pay or receive to aid in the production of the Corpus Christi Plays. The Cappers, indeed, were unusual in their desire to take over the costly business of producing a pageant.

Robert Crow

When one turns directly to the Cappers' dramatic activities it is the cost, the high cost of some kind of dramatic entertainment ten years before they take over the Cardmakers' pageant, that focuses attention very early on the single name, Robert Crow, that has represented Coventry most frequently in histories of medieval dramatic history; and Crow's name appears from 1510 until 1566 in all the extant guild records in one capacity or another in pageant production. As a Capper he is first heard of as a new brother paying wax silver to mark the end of his apprenticeship in 1510 (f. 11b).

Crow's early career was undistinguished. He was involved in some unspecified legal business with or for the Cappers in 1513 and in the same year was among the smallest contributors to one of Henry VIII's frequent calls upon Coventry for money – he gave 9d. (ff 51a/b). In seven years he advanced more quickly than any other of his fellows and became Master of the Company in 1520 (ff. 23b – 25b). In 1522 he paid licence fees for his first apprentice (his only one, it appears) (f. 29a). His problematic dramatic history begins in 1525. On Candlemas (February 2) that year the Cappers had an unusually grand entertainment which seems to have been dramatic in form. The relevant items in the account read:

Itm payed for the soteltys on Candelmas daye	vj[s]	viij[d]
Itm payd to Robert Crowe for Goldenflece	xx[s]	
Itm pd to John Crowe and Wyllyam lynes for the same	xiij[s]	iiij[d]
Itm pd to the syngers on candelmase daye	xx[d]	

---

6. These wages were set in a time of economic unrest. It is not possible to suggest standard wages for Tudor England; at different times and in different places they varied considerably.

Itm pd for suttelts	ij^s	v^d
Itm pd for payntyng the sotelts		xij^d
Itm pd to the players	iij^s	iiij^d

The accounts for the next seven years give no details of expenses, only summary totals, so that it is impossible to tell from them in what manner this entertainment was followed up, or even if it was. The occasion for the entertainment seems fairly clear. Nicholas Heynes, Master of the Cappers in 1502, and again in 1515, assumed his duties as Mayor of Coventry on February 2, 1525, having been elected, as was the custom, a week before. The Cappers, seemingly, celebrated this and apt enough symbolism in their subject of the Golden Fleece could be found for the occasion.

What exactly the "Goldenflece" was, what the painted "suttelts" were and what the relationship between them was can only be guessed at. Musicians were needed and so were players or actors. The entertainment may have been a tableau, it may have been some kind of play. The case for assuming that "players" means actors and not musicians is supported by the separate appearance of singers in the records. The case would be secure if there were in this year's accounts a payment to minstrels, but there is not. In 1513 "a mynstrell for the yere" received 3s. 4d. (f. 15b), and in 1533 3s. (f. 46a), while in 1538 there was gathered for the minstrel 3s. 8d. (f. 86a). But no minstrel or minstrels got so much for single performance as did the players in 1525. The basic items listed above (excluding various other costs for cressett light, wine and torches that may or may not be for the Candelmas celebration) amount to 48s. 5d. Except for the year when they take over control of their pageant, it is almost twenty years before the Cappers spend so much, even on the pageant. At no other time do they spend so much on entertainment for themselves.

After this enigmatic extravagance there is no further mention of Crow's name in the records of the Company. The name does occur, however, in other guild records over the next forty years and all of these references (which are more than is generally allowed) come together to produce the man who writes plays, acts in them, handles properties and costumes for plays and processions – the man who, from Sharp to Hardin Craig and Glynne Wickham, has come to represent the accomplished all-round medieval dramatic craftsman.

His chief claim to fame is as author/reviser of the two surviving plays from the Coventry Cycle, that of the Shearmen and Taylors (*The Annunciation, Nativity, Innocents*) the manuscript of which was burned at Birmingham in 1879, and that of the Weavers (*The Purification and the Doctors*) the manuscript of which, in his own hand, still survives. The former is dated 14 March, 1534 (i:e 1535) and termed by Crow "nevly correcte," the latter is dated 2 March, 1534 (i:e 1535) and termed "matter nevly translate." Available records of other companies mention no revising of their pageants at this time but, again, shorthand accounting is especially frustrating here, for the Cappers, clearly anxious to make a mark on becoming responsible for a pageant, spent lavishly on refurbishing. Only once more in their pageant history did they exceed the 1534 repairs sum of 31s. 5d. and that was in 1551 when there is some uncertainty about the meaning of the account.[7] In 1534, especially if Robert Crow the writer was the ex-Master of their company, it would have been natural that he should have prepared a new version of the play for his fellow craftsmen.

Be that as it may, the next group of references to Robert Crow fall between 1556 and 1566 (and once more, awkwardly, the very years for which no Cappers' accounts are extant). In 1557 Robert Crow was paid 20s. by the Drapers "for makyng of the boke for the paggen" (S 217, quoted from D 38a). This is a very handsome payment, for the Weavers allowed "for makyng of the play boke v^s" (Weavers A, f. 16a), which is what the Drapers themselves paid in 1568 "to ffrauncys pynnyng for a playe" (D 74a). Perhaps this sum indicates a complete rewriting as against a revision? In 1563 the Smiths paid "to Robart Croo for ij leves of ore pley boke, v:ij^d" (S 36).[8] Crow the actor is paid for God's part in 1562 and

7. In 1551 "Expensys on nwe payntyng for the pageaunt" comprising "payd for lynen clothe to paynt, v^s; payed to horseley, xxxiij^s iiij^d; payed for white incoll, x^d; payed at androes, xiiij^d; payed for makyng nwe of pylats malle, xx^d" amounted to 42s. (f. 79b). There follow the usual payments for two rehearsals but no other pageant expenses are listed. Either the pageant, after great preparation, was not given (other companies performed theirs) or, for some reason, production costs were not entered. One possible explanation is that the very large payment to Horseley was made for his painting and for his acting as pageant-master that year. It is a possibility I do not accept. Civic reiterations that pageants must be played might argue that occasional non-performances by guilds were not unknown.

8. A note at the end of the Weavers' pageant MS reads: "17 leves in all." Crow's fee was 5s. ("Itm payd for makyng of the play boke, v^s" f. 16a) which

1566 (in the latter year he also received 2d. for his gloves, as he did in 1557 when presumably his part was also that of God). In 1567 Cowtts is named as the actor of God's part and as Crow is no more named in the Drapers' records it may be safe to assume that he took no further part in their dramatic activities. The Drapers' pageant of Doomsday ended with an earthquake and the burning of the world. Whatever was the model of the world used for this climactic display, Crow seems to have been the regular maker of it: he is paid 2s. for it in 1556, and 3s. 8d. in 1561, 1563, 1566 (it is again a sample of the idiosyncratic nature of company's book-keeping that though it is, I think, fair to assume that Crow made these worlds throughout his period of attachment to the Company, it is only at the whim of the clerk whether he be named or not). In 1562 Crow is also listed as receiving 12d. "for a hat for the pharysye" (D 57a:S 72). The Drapers following the Cappers' example, and possibly trying to outdo them, occasionally paraded a giant and his wife: in 1556 Crow is named as the maker of these giants, for 1s. 8d.

I believe there were at least two Robert Crows in Coventry. He who became a full-fledged Capper in 1510 after completion of a seven-year apprenticeship must have been born about 1490 or earlier. If he wrote for the Shearmen and Taylors, he did so in his maturity. "By the mid-sixteenth century, ex-officers (of the Cappers) were being termed 'the Auncente' or 'the moost auncient persones of a craft' — designations that implied more than official seniority when 60 percent of the members of even a prosperous

---

is 7d. for two leaves. Tudor writers were paid piece-work rates, it seems, much as many modern writers are.

The quality of Crow's literary workmanship is extensively dealt with by Hardin Craig in the prefatory matter to *Two Coventry Corpus Christi Plays*, EETS, e.s. 87 (London, 1902; reprinted 1952) and in his larger survey, *English Religious Drama of the Middle Ages* (Oxford, 1955), pp. 163–166, 293–298. Craig thinks that Crow's work is "ignorant, inept and pompous . . . he spoiled a good deal of the verse, mixed up the stanza forms, and used many large words" (ERD 295). This is harsh and unfair to Crow the play-writer; concentration upon details of poetic technique obscures the fact that Crow's versions act well and that his control of theatrical language is effective. Oddly enough, Craig admits this later, but by default as it were. when he quotes a speech of the "notorious" Herod in the course of castigating the Shearmen and Taylors' play for its "bad eminence in low comedy" (ERD 297). At the same time Crow is also glanced at for his "outlandish spelling" but that seems hardly more culpable in the sixteenth century than his unexceptional use of the occasional long word. Crow's verse needs to be heard rather than read.

craft like the Cappers do not seem to have survived twenty years of membership and at a period in which 'the best age' was considered over at forty."[9] If the same man acted God's part for the Drapers in 1566, he was in his mid to late seventies at least. This seems to me improbable, no matter how suggestive of type-casting.

In summary, we have Robert Crow the Capper, Master of the Company in 1525 and no more heard of in their records thereafter: Robert Crow the reviser of the extant Coventry plays in 1534: and Robert Crow the writer, actor, properties' man for the Drapers between 1556 and 1566. It has usually been assumed that all three are one, and always that the latter two are one. The twenty-year gap after 1534, the relatively large span of time covered are awkward facts to arrange satisfactorily. Perhaps all one can say now is that it would be equally odd for one man to have so strangely sporadic a career as that two, or three, of the very few named writers, actors and producers of pageants should all be named Robert Crow – though theatrical families are not unusual. Strictly speaking the problem is insoluble at the moment but I think it should be faced. My reason for rehearsing these facts is not only that they pertain to almost the only named writer at Coventry, or anywhere else, of the Corpus Christi Plays, but that he may be the Cappers' chief claim to significance in the history of medieval drama.

Performing the Cycle

Little in the Cappers' accounts helps settle the question of how many times the cycle was performed on Corpus Christi Day in Coventry. The cycle probably consisted of ten plays, each containing material that made three or four plays at York or Chester. Ten plays of this length could not have been performed ten times each on any one day. When Queen Margaret "came prevely to the play" in 1457 she stayed at "Richard Wodes the Grocer" in Earl Street "and there all the plays were furst pleyde . . . save Domesday, which myght not be pleyde for lak of day" (Leet 300). This, however, was a special occasion despite the Queen's gracious effort at privacy, and not only was Earl Street an unusual first

9. Phythian-Adams, "Ceremony and the Citizen," p. 59. Glynne Wickham, after briefly rehearsing Crow's theatrical activities, wondered whether there might not be two men of this name, father and son (*Early English Stages*, Vol. I, 299 and 389, fn. 93).

standing but the occasion would demand fitting entertainment by Wodes of food and drink that must have quite put out the time-table of performances. The cycle could not have been so organized that the final play, especially so spectacular a one as the Drapers' Doomsday play, was likely to be dropped. I believe that the cycle generally was performed three times each year. The Drapers' accounts bear this out. They provided themselves yearly with three worlds to burn at the end of their play and it is inconceivable that, if there were ten performances (or any number more than three), all but three should have lacked this spectacle. In 1557 their pageant expenses include "aylle for the plears at thre tymes, xiiij^d" (D 39). This is the sum usually paid at this period to the drivers for drink and the next item but one above it in the same account reads: "payd to the plears when the fyrste paggen was played to drynke, ij^s." This likewise was the regular amount for the actors' drinking. None the less the important feature of the first item is the "thre tymes." These times, I think, would most naturally be after each performance, or, if drivers were intended, after the wagon has been drawn to each of its three playing places.

The Cappers' accounts are not so clear in their indications – or not so susceptible to clarity. The most direct statement, paradoxic-ally, only raises an unanswerable problem. In 1544 they "payd for drynk in the pageant for the pliars for bothe days, viij^d" (f. 62b). This is the sole reference in the Cappers' accounts to performances on two days (it does not refer to the customary two rehearsal days which are accounted for earlier in the same list). The other pay-ments for the year's pageant are the same as usual, which suggests not extra performances but performances spread over two days. There is nothing in other extant guild records to suggest that the plays were performed on two days in that year or in any other. The only other clues to the number of pageant performances come from other drinking items: there are frequent payments for drink, either "betwixt stagys" (1553, f. 84b), or, as in 1544, "drynk to the playars betwyne tyms" (f. 62b). In 1567, 1568 and 1571 the entry reads "paid to the players att the second stage" (H-P, *Outlines* I, 339–340). Does this mean that they were refreshed at the halfway mark in the show or, as it says, at the second performance of the play: if it were after the second performance could one assume at least one further performance to come? At all events the play was performed at least twice. For the remainder of the 1570s the payment is for drinking between the stages.[10]

The Writing and Revising of the Cappers' and Others' Plays

Unverifiable tradition attests to the creation of the cycle in 1416 and a revision of it in 1519. The Coventry Annals, a series of late seventeenth-century manuscripts all deriving from some lost earlier calendar, include much information about dramatic activities. They deal with real events but cast over them a legendary glaze that distorts; they all agree that in 1416, "The pageants and Hox tuesday invented, wherein the King and Nobles took great delight." No guild records survive to verify this. Henry V visited Coventry in 1416 to see the plays and possibly they were revised for the occasion. Certainly they were not "invented" then as they were in existence in 1392. In 1519 the Annals announce "New Plays at Corpus xpityde which were greatly commended." Sharp could find no corroboration of this, but he only had the Smiths' Account book to look at (the Cappers at this time were merely contributory to the Girdlers) and we know nothing of nine of the presumed ten pageants. It is possible that there were new plays in the cycle rather than a new cycle in 1519.

The Cappers presented revised if not new plays fairly frequently. A study of the payments to actors suggests at least four revisions between 1534 and 1579 (ignoring the possible rewriting or revision when they acquired the pageant). Our Lady is present in 1534 but after 1547 the part is dropped. Between 1555 and 1563 the enigmatic Mother of Death is also written out. The first payment for a Prologue is in 1573 and it is so unusual, or special, that the name of the actor (George Loe) is given. A further revision occurs in 1576 when the Deadman is introduced. His name reminds one of the Mother of Death, and the link is made the stronger because the part is tacked on to that of God and one actor is paid for both roles: and he is paid the same amount that he received for acting only God's part in 1574. In 1544 and again in 1550 God and the Mother of Death were entered as a double role, though on those occasions the actor added the 4d. received for the Mother of Death to 1s. 4d. for God and received 1s. 8d. The

---

10. "Between the stages" is the usual phrase in the Drapers', Weavers' and Smiths' accounts.

awkwardness of assessing the purpose of the Mother of Death's role is increased by the fact that in two years (1540 and 1543) her part was apparently cut from the performance.

When payments other than for actors are examined other revisions may be postulated. The slightest of them concerns Harry Person. In 1547 one penny was paid "for wrytyng apte" for him. I do not know who he is or what his part was, or whether it was a single part copied out for him to learn. Whatever the case, his career was short: in the next year two successive items read: "gyven to harrye person at the crafts desyer, xij^d" and "pd for a wynding shite for hym, xij^d" (ff. 69a, 71b).

A much grander business occurs in 1552 (see Account on page 43). "Makyng new of the plea bok" costs 5s. (The wording is virtually the same as that in the Weavers' accounts for 1535: "payd for makyng of the play boke, v^s" [f. 16a].) This item follows the puzzling "mattr of the castell of emaus" which is the most bureaucratic sounding entry in the accounts and, not surprisingly therefore, is open to various interpretations. Is it a payment for the section of the play that dealt with this incident, which then entailed the revision of the whole play to accommodate it? (In accounting for actors' wages the only effect the writing had was that the four knights increased their wages from 4s. to 4s. 8d.) Does it concern the construction of some property necessary to the play? There is nothing in the entries concerning properties and property repairs that substantiates the suggestion. Whatever the matter was and whatever the writing it occasioned, it was a Cappers' matter, for no other extant accounts mention writing or revision at this time.

The last revisions come from the period covered only by partial extracts, albeit extracts chosen, presumably, for their particular rather than their general interest. In 1563 2s. 4d. is paid "to the syngers & makynge the songe" (H-P Wb 155, p. 31). This is 12d. more than they ever received before, and the extra money doubtless paid for the song. Two years later, in 1566, a further 16d. is "payd for prikynge the songes" (H-P Wb 177, p. 31). This is rather expensive for merely copying out the music (which is usually what "prikynge" entails). Possibly a considerable amount of music was used in the pageant and it was all freshly copied out. However, in 1569, "Thomas Nyclys for prikinge the songes" was paid 12d. (S. 48). Either copies of the music are wearing out with unprecedented speed in the 1560s or there is a considerable amount of musical revision taking place. The latter seems more likely.

The period is a turbulent one in the religious history of Coventry. In 1556 Mary had to force a Catholic mayor on the city.

> The burning of several Marian martyrs strengthened the anti-Catholic and Puritan tendencies in the city, which erupted during the 1560s in an orgy of iconoclasm . . . images and relics were beaten down and burnt in the streets, organs were removed from the churches, paintings were whitewashed, and in an excess of zeal even the registers of St. Michael's were burnt because they contained "some marks of popery. . . ." Although religion in Coventry was of a strongly Protestant tone, fanatical puritanism seems to have been resisted by the majority of the population. It was, however, the creed of the ruling oligarchy and of the clergy, who would have been happy to move in the direction of a Calvinistic theocracy.[11]

Remembering this, it is likely that the Cappers were altering the songs and hymns in their pageant to fit the changing mood of the time. And it is not surprising that revisions of other pageants date from this period.

A brief summary of what is known of pageant revision in other guilds will not only set that of the Cappers in the larger framework but also introduce one more playwright in the Company.

In 1557 the Drapers, as we have seen, paid 20s. for "the boke for the paggen." This is four times the usual rate, a rate adhered to by the Drapers themselves in 1568 (see below), and suggests a very thorough rewriting. However, it entailed no alteration in the dramatis personae and asked for no new properties. If, as is possible, the Drapers were heeding Marian intervention in civic affairs they were precipitate, for in 1558 she was dead and Elizabeth was queen. Whatever the precise pressure of events, the Drapers amended their pageant again in 1561. Two new characters called "wormes of Conscyence" were added, and the whole was introduced by the "playing of the protestacyon" (D 54), in subsequent years called the Prologue. They may have gone further in revision in 1568: the last item in the "Chargys for owre pagen" for that year is "pd to ffrancys pynnyg for a playe, v^s" (D 74). As in 1557, this had no effect on characters or properties demanded.

11. Diane K. Bolton, "Social History to 1700," in *Victoria County History of Warwick*, VIII, 217–218.

Francis Pynnyg was a Capper and became Master of the Company in 1573. He would be a reasonable candidate for the author of the Cappers' revisions in 1573 and 1576.

The Weavers, after Crow revised their play, made only one alteration to their production. In 1549 the Little Child appears in their pageant accounts, and thereafter, until 1579, he (more usually his mother) is paid 4d. Probably he had nothing to say as he would be the child Jesus offered up in the temple before Simeon. Presumably a puppet was used earlier and the introduction of the living child was a touch of new dramatic realism rather than, strictly speaking, a revision. The Weavers were the most conservative of pageant producers. Perhaps because it called for no spectacle or extravagant charactery as did the Cappers', Smiths' and Drapers' pageants, the pageant was remarkably economic in its upkeep, especially when compared with the Drapers' whose conflagration for Doomsday not only was annually expensive in itself but clearly subjected their pageant wagon to great wear and tear.

For the Smiths there is more evidence of change. In 1491 their Accounts mention a "new rygenale" (or playbook). In 1495 parts for the two knights and the demon are copied out (presumably actors' speeches rather than any revision). In 1506 the "bredren and other good ffelowys toward the Orygynall" subscribed 2s. 9d. in sums of 1d. and 2d. each. In 1563, at much the time when the Cappers and Drapers were revising parts of their pageants, the Smiths paid "to Robart Croo for ij leves of ore pley boke, viij^d." Was some slight adjustment all the Smiths thought necessary? But, like the Drapers, they were later emboldened to larger revision. A "new pley" was written that dealt with the death of Judas and thereafter was played after the regular pageant of the *Trial, Condemnation* and *Crucifixion of Christ*.

The general picture, even from such relatively slender evidence (four of ten presumed plays and incomplete guild accounts of those four) is of much revising and rewriting by individual guilds. The dates of the revisions show them not to have been done in concert. Obviously a guild was not free to play fast and loose with its fragment of the Bible story, and one intent on revision may well have discussed it with other guilds and other authorities but, within the framework of the cycle, individual guilds in Coventry manipulated their pageants relatively freely.

Actors and Staging

Two notes about acting preface my final comments on actors' properties, costumes and their stage.

Apart from Harry Person and George Loe, only two actors are mentioned by name in the Cappers' accounts; they share an item in 1553. "Pd. to vaughen tht shuld have played in tompson sted, vj^d" (f. 84b). This sum was the wage for playing either "maudlyn" or one of the "ij maryes." Vaughen may have been a journeyman for his name does not appear in any quarterage list: he may not even have been a Capper at all. Tompson shortly after this became Clerk to the Company. Presumably there were regular actors for roles (as Crow for the Drapers) and stand-ins, as today, and on this occasion Vaughen came so close to acting he had to be recompensed.

The other item is undated and is pasted in a Halliwell-Phillipps' scrapbook (Wb 206, f. 63) entitled "Actresses." "Cappers Company, Coventry: The names of them that be agreyed to playe our pagyand & to be at comandement to that we shall be layd to at the quenes comynge." Then follows Halliwell-Phillipps' note, "24 names. *All men.*" The fact that they were all men is sufficient for his particular purpose but it would have been very useful to have had the names to match against the quarterage lists and other Coventry records. That twenty-four men were ready to act if called upon is interesting: the Cappers needed only fourteen men to fill the roles listed in their pageant accounts at this time. The time must have been 1565 when Queen Elizabeth visited Coventry. Ironically, the Cappers, for all their preparedness, were not chosen to exhibit their show before the queen; in the end the choice fell upon the Tanners, Smiths, Weavers and Drapers.

In addition to the scattered references to players' costumes and stage properties throughout the accounts there exist two inventories of the same, both taken from now lost originals by Halliwell-Phillipps. One dates from 1566, the other from 1597. Of the latter, he writes in his *Outlines*: "An inventory of the goods of the Cappers' Company, taken in 1597, includes – ij. pawles, sixe cressittes, ij. streamars and the poles, ij. bisshopes myters, Pylates dublit, ij. curtaynes, Pylates head, fyve Maries heades, one coyff, Mary Maudlyns gowne, iij. beardes, sixe pensils, iiij. rolles, iij Marye boxes, one playboke, the giandes head and clubbe, Pylates clubbe, hell-mowth, Adams spade, Eve's distaffe" (I, 342).[12]

The 1566 inventory is fuller and is found in the scrapbook entitled "Costumes" (Wb 150, f. 73). It reads as follows:

> The invetary of all goodes late in the custody and Kepenge of Thomas Lynycars late desesyde, takeine the iiij[th] of Marche, 1566, before Nycolas Harvy, John Howes & John Grenne, & dellyveryde to the handes of Thomas Harvy the day & yere abovesaid.

Pagaunte vestneres

Item, ij stremars & pensells
Item, Mawdlen Kertell; Pyllutes dublyt.
Item, ij byshopes cottes with ther hoodes; j pere of sleeves
Item, ij albes hodes Pyllutes hede
Item, ij byshopes mytteres
Item, iij Maeryes hede, the Spyrytes of Godes cote
Item, Godes hede & hys cote & Sperytes hede
Item, ij cortenus the dymons cote & his hed
Item, iij folles hedes
Item, Godes crose & the Spyrytes crose
Item, Pylates mawlle & his clobe
Item, a dystaff & a spade
Item, vij cressetes & viij coltes to them
Item, a baskete & a boxe
Item, a wrynles & a cord to the stevenne
Item, iiij Kofferes
Item, ij Maryes Koyffes
Item, more, iiij lyly pennes for the whelles
Item, more, ix fannes
Item, more, iij Maryes boxes
v small stremers
ix faynes with iron steyles
Godes apparne of red say
Paynted clothes for the pagent.

The 1597 inventory, whether complete or merely excerpted, shows what was left years after the cycle was performed; the 1566 one lists what was used while productions were current. That being so, it is odd that the hellmouth, the "playboke," "iij beardes"

12. Sharp quotes similar inventory from Lincoln of 1564 (S62) but seems to have been unaware of the Cappers' 1566 one. He refers to a Cappers' inventory of 1590 and quotes two items from it: "sixe cressites ij streamers and the poles &c" (S185). I think this the inventory H-P dates 1597. Of the bishops' gear only the mitres remain after the sale of their hoods and fur in 1596, therefore I prefer 1597 to 1590.

and "iiij rolles" listed in 1597 are not mentioned. They must have been kept by someone other than Lynycars. "The giandes head and clubbe" turns up even more unexpectedly in 1597: it is not pageant stuff but to do with the giant that was carried in the Midsummer and St. Peter's processions between 1533 and 1562.

Space allows comment on only one or two items from the earlier list. Sharp mentions "that in an inventory of Ornaments, Jewels, Goods, &c. belonging to the Cappers' Chapel, 28 Henry VIII, the following entry occurs: – 'It, ij pajiont Clothes of the passion,' and a conjecture is hazarded that these clothes, whether painted or tapestry work, were displayed on the Vehicle or used for covering the lower room of it, at the time of representing the Cappers' Pageant" (S47–48). The inventories support this conjecture. Halliwell-Phillipps mentions the same Chapel clothes and adds that "in a list of the theatrical appliances of another trading company, 1565, are included 'three paynted clothes to hang abowte the pageant.' Some of the pageant accounts include payments 'for curten ryngus' " (Outlines II, 289). The Cappers' "paynted clothes" were probably hung from the wagon stage to cover the wheels while the "ij cortenus" were used on-stage.[13]

All the named characters wore "hedes" or masks (but not the angels, knights and bishops; the Mother of Death was dropped before 1566 and the Deadman does not appear until 1576). Who wore the "iij folles hedes" is problematical. Possibly their wearers – otherwise unnamed in the accounts – abetted Pilate in his comedy with the mall and leather balls. The 1597 inventory includes "fyve Maries heades" which suggests either that spares were kept or that five rather similar masks were arbitrarily lumped together by the 1597 inventory-taker: were the "folles hedes" spares? It is even possible that Halliwell-Phillipps misread "s" as "f" and these are three "solles" masks for characters who may have taken a part in *The Harrowing of Hell*. That these characters, whether "folles" or "solles," are never listed in the payments to actors is not unusual and introduces another puzzle in the Cappers' (and the Weavers') accounts.

13. H-P's unnamed company is not the Weavers', Drapers' or Smiths', although his sense suggests he is referring to a Coventry company. "Curten ryngus" are found in the Smiths' accounts: tenterhooks, also for hanging clothes and curtains, are found in all extant Coventry companies' records. A brief discussion (with illustrations) of clothes and curtains on pageant-wagons can be found in Wickham, *Early English Stages* I, 172–174.

The Cappers' inventories show that Adam and Eve, though never mentioned in the accounts, played in the pageant. If they did not speak and were identified by the spade and distaff they carried, doubling may account for their non-appearance in the accounts. Interesting light is thrown on this matter when the Weavers' play is compared with their accounts for it. The two Prophets who introduce their play in a passage of 176 lines are never mentioned in the company's accounts, nor are the three Doctors who question the child Christ in the temple and have parts of 85, 45 and 38 lines, nor is Gabriel who speaks 22 lines. To fit up a doubling scheme to take care of these omissions is possible but one is then left with actors having lengthy double roles and being paid astonishingly little for them compared with the wages paid to other actors of leading roles. Simeon's Clerk is regularly given wages, but the stage directions always refer to Clerks in the plural and Simeon so addresses them at times. From 1549 to 1579 "the lettell chyld" has a role. I think he did not speak; but, if a part was written in for him, there is no sign of it in the extant manuscript which has various marks and notes in later sixteenth-century hands than Crow's. Thus, the light thrown on the problem of the number of actors needed by a play, and the number of roles they took, and the basis upon which they were paid, is of the sort that reveals the complexity of that problem rather than provides any solution. As the Cappers' records show, doubling by the actor of God's part role did not always add to his wages.

Where costumes are concerned nothing is entered for the knights because their armour was hired each year. The bishops' "cottes with ther hoodes" are gone in 1597 because they were sold in 1596: the fur for 14d. and the hoods for 8s. to Richard Dabson, sometime Master of the Cappers (f. 134b). They were prized garments and had been more expensively maintained than any others. In 1550 their making cost 2s. 4d. and their furring 2s. 4d. (f. 77b); in 1565 "dressynge & colorynge" the hoods cost 2s. and furring them another 8s. (S 49–50); the next year "an ell of bockram for one of the byshoppes" – a clumsy actor? – cost 14d. (H-P, Wb 177, p. 31).

The pageant wagon was not only finely and artistically decorated but most carefully cared for. In being pulled through the rough narrow streets and used to stage what was not one of the quieter plays it suffered much wear and tear. Almost yearly there are minor things to be set right wanting nails, boards and iron-work.

Frequently major repairs are needed. In 1543 two men spent a day on the sides of the wagon and the scaffolds while "kepton the smythe" put a new wheel on the pageant and generally strengthened all the pageant and scaffold wheels (f. 58a). Another 3s. 4d. was expended the next year, primarily on the scaffolds (f. 63a), and the same sum was paid in 1548 for iron work on the wagon and wheels (f. 72a). In 1553 a new pair of trestles (20d.) and "byndyng" a wheel cost together 7s. 6d. (f. 84b). The missing years show a new wheel in 1565 (S 49) and much work for carpenter and smith in 1569 (5s. 8d.: H-P Wb 177, p. 52). In every year from 1573 until 1579 (there was no performance due to plague in 1575) there were expensive wagon repairs. Two carpenters worked two days on it and the scaffolds in 1573 (f. 106a); a single carpenter put in a day and a half, mainly on the scaffolds, in 1574 (f. 108a); two carpenters spent a day using up 5s. 6d. worth of "bordes, ledgis (and) carte nayles" on general maintenance in 1576 (f. 111b). In the last three years of performance "good man malpas" the wheelwright was steadily employed. He attended "the oversight off the pagyn wheles" in 1577 (f. 113b), supplied "ij newe skaffolde wheles" for 6s. 8d. in 1578 (f. 115a), and received 5s. for "a newe pagyn whele" in 1579 (f. 116b).

Whatever the ill omens for the continuing production of the Corpus Christi Play in Coventry in the seventies, the Cappers' accounts show no falling off in money spent on the upkeep of their own pageant, no signs of unease or dwindling interest. Mysteries' actual end in Coventry was sharp and sudden. But it is no more fully and clearly explicable for all that.

A hard-headed man once expostulated: "Yes, I have a pair of eyes, and that's just it. If they wos a pair o' patent double million magnifyin' gas microscopes of hextra power, p'raps I might be able to see through a flight o' stairs and a deal door; but bein' only eyes, you see my wision's limited." The limitations of my vision have been obvious, limited not only by the mode of the Cappers' accounting but by the four-hundred-year gap between their reports and these glosses on some items in those reports. "What is truth?" asked jesting Pilate; the Cappers' Pilate seems to have had a bent towards raucous humour rather than philosophical questioning, but he, and that "seems to have had," are a further reminder that in writing about what has been called "true Coventry," I do not pretend to have brought *the* truth about Coventry's plays or even the Cappers' own play and its production, but, at best, to have rephrased some of the questions that will eventually have to be answered if that elusive truth is to be found. In the finding Sam Weller's cry leads me to my final note and last puzzle. A flight of stairs I cannot produce, although in 1576 2s. was "paide ffor iiij iorn clyppes ffor the wheles and shuttinge the howkes for the ladder" (f. 111b). But a door I cannot quite see through I can produce. Also in 1576 12d. was "paide for a dore and hynges and nayles behynd the pagyn" (f. 111b). It is just possible that this refers to a stage door, an actors' entrance on to the pageant-wagon stage rather than a pageant-house door.

Pageant-house doors are often mentioned: in 1555 "pd for mendyng of the pageant house dore, vj^d" (f. 94b), "pavynge affore the pagyn howse dore" cost 4d. in 1581 (f. 119a). The doors were mended in 1593 (f. 132a), 1598 (f. 137a), 1605 (f. 143a), and 1617 (f. 155a). These are the large doors that open wide to receive the wagon and scaffolds. "The dore . . . behynd" must, if it is not a stage door, be a rear door to the pageant-house and one mentioned nowhere else. It must be admitted that "bordes to mende the pagyn dores" and "newe cordes to make ffaste owre pagyn dores" in 1579 seem to refer to pageant-house doors (f. 116b). A year later 6d. was "payde ffor mendynge the pagyn dores that boyes had opened and ffor settynge in off the skaffolde" (f. 118a). Again it is likelier that the boys forced the front large doors than that they entered by the pageant-house windows (often enough repaired, as it happens, over the years) and forced a door on the wagon itself? Where evidence about the actual stage for the pageant plays is so slight, an attempt to see through the "dore behynd" should be made.

However, the last word should not be with unruly boys and back doors. References to the pageant-house occur in the Cappers' accounts until 1630 when they gave up possession of it to one Mr. Jesson. The old name recurring in their accounts was a reminder into Caroline times of pageant-playing days and of the fact that when the plays were silenced in the city the names and memories associated with them were not.[14]

14. My full-scale study of medieval dramatic entertainments in Coventry is currently in preparation: the documentary evidences will appear as part of the Malone Society Collections Series. The research for this paper was supported by grants from the Canada Council and UBC Research Fund.

APPENDIX:

Cappers' Accounts for 1534:

Exspenc for the yere

first payed to whyrrett for standyng		
of or pageant		iiij^{d}
It pd for vij ston of Cresset lyght	ij^{s}	iiij^{d}
Itm pd for beryng the same and		
Cressetts		x^{d}
It pd for Dryssyng the gyant		vj^{d}
It pd for beryng the gyant		xij^{d}
It pd for naylls & Corde		ij^{d}
Itm pd for ponts		j^{d}
Itm pd two mynstrells	iiij^{s}	
Spent at the kyngs hede on the		
Company		xiij^{d}
[these are the first 9 items in a longer list]		
Repacons made of the pageant and		
players Ger	xxxj^{s}	v^{d}ob
ffirst payed for two Rehersys	ij^{s}	iiij^{d}
Itm pd to pylate	iij^{s}	viij^{d}
Itm pd to the Syngers		xvj^{d}
Itm payed to god		xvj^{d}
Itm payed to mother of deth		iiij^{d}
Itm payed to foure knyghtes	iiij^{s}	
It payed to the sprett of god		xv^{d}
Itm payed to oure lady		xij^{d}
Itm payed to two bysshopps	ij^{s}	
Itm payed to two awngells		viij^{d}
Itm payed to mare magdeleyn		xij^{d}
Item payed to two syde maryes		xij^{d}
Itm payed to the demon		xvj^{d}
Itm payed to the mynstrell		viij^{d}
Itm payed for the players supp	ij^{s}	
Itm payed for drynke to the dryvers		
of the pageant		viij^{d}
Itm payed for foure harnesse		xvj^{d}
Itm payed for dressyng the pageant		viij^{d}
Itm payed for v dossan ponts		iiij^{d}
Itm payed for Rysshes		j^{d}

Itm payed to lewez for drynvyng
    the pageant   vj^d

Itm payed for mete and drynke to
    the players at the Swane   vj^d

Spent at the dryvyng owte the
    pageant   vj^d

Spent at the bryngyng yn the
    pageant   vj^d

Itm payed for gloves   xx^d

                              S̄m   xxx^s iiij^d [actually 30/8]

Cappers' Accounts for 1552 (Thomas Myddleton, master):

payments for the pagyon

    spent at the fyrst rehers of the plears   xviij^d
    spent at borseley at the Said rehers   ij^s
    pd to the plears at the second rehers   xviij^d
    spent at the Said rehers   xx^d

    for mendyng of the skaffold
    pd for a quarter pesse   vj^d
    pd for a boord   vj^d
    pd for nailles   iij^d
    pd to the wryghts   vij^d
    pd for clamps of Iorn   iiij^d
    pd for tenterhooks   j^d
    pd for vj^d nailles   j^d
    pd for sope   ij^d

    The plears wages
    pd to pylatt   iiij^s viij^d
    pd to god   xvj^d
    pd to the mother of death   iiij^d
    pd to the spyrt of god   xvj^d
    pd to maudlyn   xij^d
    pd to the ij marys   xij^d
    pd to the ij byschopps   ij^s
    pd to the iiij knyghts   iiij^s
    pd to the ij angells   viij^d
    pd to the demon   xvj^d

pd to the syngers		xvj^d
pd to the mynstrell		viij^d
pd for the plears Supp	ij^s	
pd for the hyer of harnes		xx^d
pd for dryvyng the pagen and for drynk to the plears		xx^d
pd to viij men tht dryved the pagyon		xvj^d
pd to the wryght for tendyng the wynd		ix^d
pd for vj dessen of poynts		xij^d
pd for gloves	ij^s	iiij^d
pd for settyng in of the pagen		iij^d
pd for drynk at the settyng owt & Settyng in of the pagyon		xij^d
pd for Russches		iij^d
pd for the matt^r of the castell of emaus		xiij^d
pd for makyng nwe of the plea bok	v^s	
Sum	xlvj^s	iiij^d

Cappers' Accounts for 1578
(received from Walkers 6/-, from Skinners 4/-, from Joiners 3/4)

charges off the pagyn

paide the players at the ffirst Reherse		xviij^d
spent on the company at the same Reherse	ij^s	
paide the players at the seconde Reherse		xx^d
spente on the company at the same Reherse	ij^s	
spente at the settinge fowthe off the pagyn		vj^d
paide good man malpas ffor ij newe skaffolde wheles	vj^s	viij^d
spente at the Reparynge off the pagyn		xij^d
paide ij carpenters ffor one dayes worke		xviij^d
paide ffor wasshinge the vestures		j^d
paid James bursley ffor one newe clyppes and showting off ij		viij^d
paide ffor sope ffor the wheles		iiij^d
paide ffor greate nayles small nayles and taynter howkes		ix^d

43

paide ffor hyre off harnysses ffor the pagyn
and weppons $\quad$ ij^s
spente at the settinge in off the pagyn $\qquad$ vj^d
$\qquad$ the some is xxj^s ij^d

paymentes to the players
paide ffor the prologe $\qquad$ iiij^d
paide god and the deade man $\qquad$ xx^d
paide pylate $\qquad$ iiij^s
paide the ij bysshoppes $\qquad$ ij^s
paide iiij knyghtes $\qquad$ vj^s $\quad$ viij^d
paide the spirit off god $\qquad$ xvj^d
paid iij maries $\qquad$ ij^s
paid ij angells $\qquad$ viij^d
paide the devell $\qquad$ xviij^d
paide the syngers $\qquad$ ij^s
paide the mynstrell $\qquad$ viij^d
payde ffor balls $\qquad$ xij^d
paid ffor gloves and poyntes $\qquad$ iiij^s $\quad$ vj^d
paide pylate and the iiij knyghtes to dryncke
betwene the stages $\qquad$ ix^d
paide ffor dryncke in the pagyn $\qquad$ xij^d
paide ffor dressynge off the pagyn $\qquad$ vj^d
paide ffor dryvynge off the pagyn $\qquad$ vj^s $\quad$ viij^d
paide the players ffor their supper $\qquad$ ij^s $\quad$ viij^d
paide ffor mendinge pylates gowne and his
clubbe $\qquad$ vj^d
paid ffor ffor [*sic*] the maisters supper and his
company $\qquad$ iii^s
paid ffor Russhes ffor the pagyn $\qquad$ iiij^d
$\qquad$ the some is ij^{li} $\quad$ iiij^s $\quad$ ix^d

Methods of Presentation in Pre-Shakespearian Theatre

RICHARD SOUTHERN

Dr. Richard Southern's unscripted talk with this title consisted of a summary of the longer study published in his new book The Staging of Plays before Shakespeare. *This talk was explained by a series of blackboard drawings that grew during the session. Rather than attempt to reduce his demonstration to essay form we print an extract from the above-mentioned book especially edited and illustrated by the author (by kind permission of the publishers Messrs. Faber and Faber).*

The anonymous Interlude of *Apius and Virginia* of about 1560 includes one of the earliest acting-directions in printed Interludes referring to the use of a stage. The word employed there is "scaffold" and the full direction reads "Here let Virginius go about the scaffold." (See the line marked with an asterisk in the analysis of the play which follows.)

For reasons given elsewhere in my book I believe this "scaffold" is likely, on some occasions, to have been a small "footpace" or rostrum, some one foot high, placed before the centre one of the typical three screens in a Tudor Hall and between the two "doors" by which the players entered the acting-area of the hall floor. For illustration see the accompanying diagram, where the details of a Tudor Hall are given in thick lines. The "traverse" shown in the diagram is included only as a suggested solution to the problem raised in *Godly Queen Hester* (c. 1527) by the direction "Here the Kynge entryth the trauers & aman goeth out" (see my book, p. 264). It would not be essential to a presentation of *Apius and*

Richard Southern

Virginia – unless, of course, advantage were taken of it to stage the trick entrance of Conscience and Justice to Judge Apius in the passage from fol. C.i. quoted below. An analysis of the whole plot of *Apius and Virginia* now follows with special emphasis on the passage containing the significant stage-direction.

A facsimile of *Apius and Virginia* was published by the Tudor Facsimile Text Society in 1908. The title-page reads as follows:

A new Tragicall Comedie
of Apius and Virginia,
Wherein is liuely expressed a rare
example of the vertue of Chastitie,
by Virginias constancy, in wishing
rather to be slaine at her owne Fa-
thers handes, then to be deflow-
red of the wicked Iudge
Apius.
By R. B.

The Players names.

Virginius.	Conscience.
Mater.	Iustice.
Virginia.	Claudius.
Haphazard.	Rumour.
Mansipulus.	Comforte.
Mansipula.	Rewarde.
Subseruus.	Doctrina.
Apius.	Memorie.

Imprinted at London, by Wil-
liam Howe, for Richard Ihones.
1575.

The action opens with a rhapsodic, even sentimental, scene between Virginius and his wife and their daughter Virginia, in which they extol their own virtuous states for five pages. Next comes a scene between Haphazard, the Vice, and three servants containing many obscurities and lasting six pages. Then Judge Apius enters and soliloquizes upon the strength of his unsatisfied lust for Virginia; Haphazard suggests a way in which Apius can seduce her. Apius is torn with doubts, and there follows this strange direction, printed in the margin:

C.i.   Here let him make as thogh he went out and let Consince and
        Iustice come out of him, and let Consience hold in his hande a
        Lamp burning and let Iustice haue a sworde and hold it before
        Apius brest.

Some editors clearly believe this direction needs amending. In
Hazlitt's Dodsley we have the suggestion of "come after him" instead of "come out of him." It might seem to meet the case better if
we simply read "come *in* to him" – implying that as Apius was on
the point of leaving, he was intercepted by two strange figures who
then performed a mimed by-play. But it is possible to retain the
direction as it stands if we go a step further, and permit ourselves
the slightly novel theory that a piece of neat trick-dodging took
place here, and that as Apius blocked the doorway with his body,
two actors simultaneously stepped from either side the door beyond him, to stand momentarily masked by him, one behind the
other, facing him in close proximity, so that he recoiled a pace and
then they side-stepped to left and right of him and so appeared to
"come out of him." This may well be possible though it seems a
little strained; it is however, in my opinion, a less unlikely interpretation than that the two appeared from below by means of some
sort of trap.

Apius' speech following their appearance has some points of
interest. He has just been announcing his intention to go and wreak
his worst on Virginia whatever happens, when these two figures
appear, and his speech at this point suddenly has the lines –

    But out I am wounded, how am I deuided?
    Two states of my life, from me are now glided, [. . .]

– and thus we seem to be given a very strong hint that in fact some
sort of trick-appearance for Conscience and Justice was engin-
eered, by which they would seem to have "glided" out from him.
Haphazard, seeming not to see them, persuades Apius that the two
figures (who have not so far spoken) "are but thoughts," and at
length Apius reaffirms his intention to "deflower hir youth," and
orders Haphazard to "Come on procede and wayte on me." Haphazard makes a curious reply, followed by two curious directions:

    At hand (quoth picke purse) here redy am I,
    See well to the [? *thee*] Cut Purse, be ruled by me.
                            Exit.   Go out here.

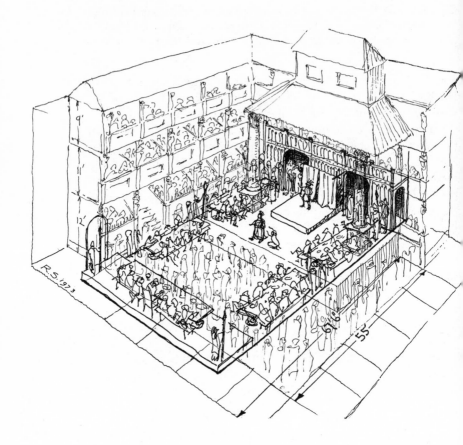

This diagram shows: (1) In thicker line, a performance in a typical Great Hall approximately 38 ft. wide and 68 ft. long, roughly the dimensions of the hall at Penshurst Place, Kent. Illustrated are the screens, a traverse with a small 'footpace', the high table opposite on a dais, the spectators sitting at side tables and standing at the screens. (2) Around this is drawn, in thinner line but *to the same scale*, a sketch of the interior of the square Fortune Playhouse based on measurements taken from the builder's contract. It will be remarked how similar the essential dimensions are. The stage is only 2 ft. 6 ins. wider, either side, than the hall; the open yard itself is 55 ft. across either way against the 38 ft. width of the hall. But chiefly the length from the screens to the back of the boxes, or 'rooms', is almost exactly the same in both. Thus, an occupant of the front box at the Fortune would sit in just the same relation to the main performance as the Lord of the House at Penshurst – but the stage of the Fortune was only 27 ft. 6 ins. deep against the full length of the hall floor available to a player at Penshurst. The drawing is made so that the hall floor is represented as raised to the level of the stage.

The reason for the two directions in different languages but with the same meaning is not clear.

Conscience and Justice, now left alone, have two short speeches (this is the first time we have heard their voices), and then they "Exit." Haphazard returns. Then (on fol. C.i.) "Here entreth Judge Apius and Claudius," and these two lay the plot mentioned earlier, that is, that Claudius should depose that Virginia had really been stolen by Virginius and was not his true daughter. Haphazard and Claudius then leave Apius who speaks three lines alone, and then there is the curious direction, "Here let Conscience speake within," and his voice now reproves Apius. Apius exclaims, "Whence doth this pinching sounde desende!" and Conscience announces his name, but says he is "Compeld to crie with trimbling soule" because he is near dying. Still Apius is unrepentant. It is, I think, clear from the elaboration of the above little scene that some particular care was taken in its presentation to make the action dramatically effective. The means may have been crude, but the technical aims of the developing Interluders seem certainly to be growing more ambitious.

Now, after a sort of break for relief, in which a song from two semi-comic servants is sung, the plot presses on with the entry of Virginius. He tells the audience that he suspects evil because of certain omens he has seen, and concludes by heralding an entrance with these words,

D.i.*rev.*   I enter will Judge Apius gate, reiecting care and mone:
          But stay Virginius, loe, thy Prince doth enter into place,
          Oh sufferant Lord, and rightfull Judge, the Gods do saue
            thy grace,
                    Here entreth Judge Apius and Claudius.

They enter from the "gate" (or door) "into place," so it would seem that they must come in on the floor level, and then they would presumably mount the stage to Virginius. Apius there delivers six lines of polite welcome to Virginius, but also informs him that he must meet an accusation. Virginius has six lines of response (including the remarkable couplet, "If ought I haue offended you, your Courte, or eke your Crowne, / From lofty top of Turret hie, persupetat me downe:") and Apius thereupon calls on Claudius to speak out. So Claudius says (I give the passage in full without

interruptions, but adding five footnotes at the end, and marking the
essential line with an asterisk):

CLAUDIUS.

Thou sufferant Lord, and rightfull Judge, this standeth now ye case,
In tender youth not long agone, nere sixtene yeares of space,
Virginius a thrall of mine, a childe and infant yonge,
From me did take by subtell meane, and keepes by arme full strong
And here before your grace I craue, that Justice be exstended,
That I may haue my thrall agayne, and faultes may be amended

VIRGINIUS.

Ah Gods that guide the globe aboue what forged tales I here,
Oh Judge Apius, bend your eares, while this my crime I cleare:
She is my child, and of my wife her tender corpes did springe,
Let all the countrey where I dwell, beare witnesse of the thing.
    Apius and Claudius go forth, but Apius speaketh this.[1]
Nay by the Gods not so my friend, I do not so decree,
I charge thee here in paine of death, thou bring the maide to mee:
In chamber close, in prison sound, the secret shall abide,
And no kinde of wight shall talke to her, vntill the truth be tride:
This doo I charge, this I commaund, in paine of death let see,
Without any let, that she be brought, as prisoner vnto me: Exit.
°   Here let Virginius go about the scaffold[2]
Ah fickle, faule, vnahppy dome, oh most vncertaine rate,
That euer chaunce so churlishly, that neuer staide in state:
What Judge is this: what cruell wretch? what faith doth Claudius
    finde?
The Gods do recompence with shame, his false and faithles minde:
Well home I must,[3] no remedy, where shall my soking teares,
Augment my woes, decrease my ioyes, while death do rid my feares
            Here entreth Rumour.[4]
        Come Ventus come, blow forth thy blast,
            Prince Eol listen well,
        The filthiest fackte that euer was,
            I Rumor now shall tell: . . .

[Rumour speaks on for twenty-four more lines, explaining Apius's
intention to deflower Virginia under pretence of questioning her
privately; then Virginius, apparently hearing this,[5] has the following
speech:]

VIRGINIUS.

O man, O mould, oh mucke, O clay, O Hell, O hellish hounde,
A faulse Judge Apius wrablinge wretch, is this thy treason found:
Woe worth the man that gaue the seede, wherby ye first didst spring

Woe worth the wombe yt bare the babe, to meane this bluddy thing:
Woe worth the paps that gaue ye sucke, woe worth the Fosters eke
Woe worth all such as euer did, thy health or liking seeke:
Oh that the graued yeares of mine, were couered in the clay
       Here entreth Virginia.

NOTES

1. The action involved here would seem to be as follows: after the accusation is made by Claudius, Claudius and Apius are directed to "go forth." This is a little surprising because, immediately afterwards, Apius has a further speech to Virginius. The suggestion is that they make *as if* to go out (possibly stepping off the stage to go to the door), but then Apius checks, turns back where he stands, and addresses a further six ominous lines to Virginius before turning again to leave. After that he has a separate, and this time unmistakable, direction to exit.

2. Now comes the direction to Virginius to "go about the scaffold." (I take it that "scaffold" means "stage.") It is easy to understand that Virginius is disturbed by this open threat to his daughter's honour, but this alone seems an insufficient reason to direct him specifically to pace to and fro. He might rage, admittedly, but to order him to stride about as he rages seems unnecessary; it is not wrong, but surely the action is a matter for his own decision! If, however, the direction is inserted to show that he too should now *leave* the stage, and rage on the floor round about that stage (and perhaps up and down the hall), then we can see at once that such an action exactly prepares the way for the entrance of Rumour, who would be free to deliver the 28-line speech about Apius's evil intentions from the empty stage while Virginius on the floor stands horrified.

A technical precedent for such an action is exactly offered in the well-known direction from the Coventry cycle, "Here Erode ragis in the pagond and in the strete also." Again, a somewhat similar situation so far as relates to an advance forward from the screens-end towards the centre of the hall, occurred in *Wit and Science* when – though for a very different reason – Wit was given the direction "Wyt cumth before." There is furthermore a similar intention suggested in a direction in *Susanna* where the two lascivious Elders "go afore into the Orchard and Susanna and her two maydes come vpon the stage."

3. Before Rumour enters, Virginius, near the end of his first diatribe against Apius, has the line "home I must"; he is therefore clearly on the point of leaving just as Rumour appears. One pictures him about to go out by one of the screens-doors when he is checked by Rumour's sudden appearance, and he stops and watches over his shoulder.

4. Rumour has run in, presumably by the door opposite to that Virginius is approaching and mounts the stage to deliver the speech, denouncing Apius.

5. During the latter part of this speech Virginius probably stands by the side of the stage taking in its full import. When it is finished, Rumour steps off the stage and goes out again, and Virginius now turns back and redoubles his diatribe in even stronger terms against the would-be violator, probably raging "about" again. At the peak of his protest his daughter comes out from the door he had been approaching and asks what it all means.

Virginius explains the whole grim situation to her and in the end, perplexed in the extreme, they can see no alternative but to take her life. So, he draws his sword and (see fol. D.iii, *rev.*) "Here let him profer a blowe"; she checks him with the ancient pretext, "Let first my wimple bind my eyes" . . . The stage direction then follows, "Here tye a handcarcher aboute hir eyes, and then strike of hir heade." This is closely reminiscent of the Tibetan procedure as described by Marion Duncan in his *Harvest Festival Dramas of Tibet*, where a character is killed by her headdress being sliced off with a sword.

I presume that the effect in *Apius and Virginia* would not have been entirely realistic, but it probably indicated what was meant well enough for that barnstorming atmosphere. What is more of a question is how the players got rid of Virginia's "headless" body. We learn that her father is told (by Comfort of all people!) to take her head to the rapacious King Apius as earnest that she preferred death to dishonour, but no indication is to be found in the script of how her body was cleared away. It may well have been, in view of the character of the rest of the play, that the lad who was playing her simply rose to his feet and walked off out of the action. Exactly that sort of solution is managed with complete propriety and unbroken dignity by the Kathakali players after one of their bloodthirsty murder scenes.

The general tenor of *Apius and Virginia* is one which amply demonstrates that the sort of action offered in the players' scene in *Hamlet* is no exaggeration.

It may be worth noting in passing that the introduction of a stage into the Interluders' technique will have one inevitable result on the character of the Interlude as an entertainment; and that is that never again can a show of this sort, presented at a banquet in a hall, effectively pretend to be a spontaneous thing. The "interlude" is finished. That engaging joke of unpremeditation that Medwall played at the beginning of the century in his *Nature* and his *Fulgens* can never be effective again. The reason being, of course, that the players could not involve a hall in the clutter and preparation of putting up a stage without giving away to the guests the fact that they were going to do a play there.

Thus, the very "interlude" nature of an Interlude must henceforward be changed; it now becomes a clearly premeditated entertainment. And it is not surprising that about this time there begins to be a distinction between the terms "Interlude" and "stage-play" as applying to two different kinds of show; and eventually both those names give way to the more specific "comedy" or "tragedy."

"Fair is foul and foul is fair": Vice-Comedy's Development and Theatrical Effects

J. A. B. SOMERSET

As recently as fifteen years ago the morality play after 1500 was regarded condescendingly, its history was seen as one of degeneration (J. M. Manly's "evolution" in reverse), and it attracted little serious attention from producers or critics. That this has changed is largely due to some of the members of this conference. While we do not today claim that the morality play is great art, we do see its history as one of change, experiment and commitment. This is especially true of the period from 1480 to 1540, during which great developments occurred due to such pressures as, theatrically, the rise of touring professional actors, and extradramatically, the Renaissance of learning and the Reformation. We also view these plays as plays for the theatre – the first truly commercial theatre in England.

The drama did not mature, but remained rough and unsubtle in dramaturgy while reflecting fervent, sometimes doctrinaire, commitments. After about 1500 only the morality plot commonly called the "psychomachia" continues to appear (while we may use the term, we should consider this plot as does Professor Robert A. Potter, as centred upon man and his life-sequence of innocence-fall-redemption, rather than as an epic battle between virtues and vices for man's soul[1]). The playwrights turn to new interests and

---

1. "The Idea of a Morality Play," *Research Opportunities in Renaissance Drama*, XIII–XIV (1970–71), 240.

subject-matter, attempting to bring this conventional plot to bear upon new and troubling problems such as worldly prosperity, just government, or right religion. At base, the writers were attempting to give a shape to the perennial problem, how do good and evil co-exist (or, rather, exist together)? Given that they do, how does one act rightly in this world, and how is action to be judged? Such problems are of vital concern in the lives of the morality heroes as also, I think, to their creators.

Professor Ingram's title admirably describes this conference's aim, of "finding the players," and this is my ultimate purpose as well, although I am approaching the task from another direction. Along with playing places, methods of troupe organization, and so on, a main influence upon the actors was their play texts, and today I wish to focus upon these with special attention to some aspects of the vice-group – the reasons for their being comically depicted, their increasing importance as a group, and their re-organization which gives rise to the "Vice" figure. The inter-dependence of playwrights and actors, and the important effects of theatrical conventions upon troupe formation will, I hope, become apparent.

The great amount of low comedy and entertainment in most of the surviving morality plays has dismayed many critics (one surmises that this is why it is ignored in some accounts of the genre). Two views have evolved regarding this comedy, the first (and, generally, older) of which regards it as "comic relief," added to the serious themes to please a rural or uneducated audience or relieve the tedium of the moral didactics. Beyond serving as a relief from piety, such comic relief often is held to nullify the professed intentions of the plays, leading to a view of it as "perhaps the most active agency in the degeneration of the morality play."[2] A second view is more sympathetic to the play's unity, and suggests that the comedy is functional in the plays' didacticism, either as satire or as a symbol of evil. "There is no such thing as innocent merriment," writes one critic, who argues that the playwrights' moral intentions are operable in all aspects of their plays.[3] This is usefully correct-ive, reminding us that the purveyors of the comic routines are characters instrumental to the moral message and that the humour

2. Hardin Craig, *English Religious Drama* (Oxford, 1955), p. 380.
3. Bernard Spivack, *Shakespeare and the Allegory of Evil* (New York, 1958), p. 121.

affects our response to the plays as wholes. Its proper function, in this view, is to reinforce the pietism of the virtues which condemns comedy *per se* as frivolous or damnable. But one wonders if this supplies a complete answer, and if comedy is to be considered as always evil because it proceeds from evil characters. Do we not at times respond to humour on its own terms? Critics generally agree that some passages of vice humour, dance or music are predominantly charming, but if we hold that comedy can be *only* a symbol of evil we must necessarily consider the charm to be an inadvertent effect, at odds with the moral purpose.[4] Perhaps the writer is not being honest with himself or with us, since he introduces passages which are, apparently, comic relief. If he allows us to laugh either in sympathy with the vice humorists or in disengagement from the plot, has he necessarily weakened his play?

One encounters a remarkable range of comic effects in the moralities. On the one hand, the sequence whereby each successive vice in *All for Money* is vomited forth by the one preceding him (11. 250 ff.) probably wins the prize for scabrous grotesquerie, while on the other hand amusement is the main effect of, say, Nichol Newfangle's revelation of his apprenticeship as a tailor in *Like Will to Like*. Professor Spivack enumerates:

> brawls . . . lascivious toys . . . profane witticisms . . . sudden and grotesque entrances, shoving aside of the audience . . . insults, scabrous language, profanity, long speeches of pure fustian, puns, malapropisms, garbled proclamations, *doubles entendres*, elegant foreignisms, and endless jests about anatomy, virginity, marriage, and the gallows.[5]

One wonders if such diverse comic routines can be called either simply horrifying or delightful. Rather, it appears that the vices neither constantly reveal themselves as fun-makers nor continually present themselves as evil. Also notable is the varying emphasis put upon humour by different playwrights. *The Contract of a Marriage Between Wit and Wisdom* admittedly veers towards sheer fun, and the low comedy seems to run away with the play.

4. Ibid., p. 218. Compare p. 113, where he argues that "the unregenerate instincts of playwright and audience maintained a running quarrel" with the moral seriousness of the plays, and so farcical stage business and humour were supplied to hold "the allegiance of mere flesh and blood."
5. Ibid., p. 117.

On the other hand, John Bale's *Three Lawes* or Nathanial Woodes' *The Conflict of Conscience* avail themselves of little comedy, and depict their vices as grotesque. Between these extremes there is, I think, a mean – a usual mode of characterization and plot development which mingles the comedy of evil and the comedy of appeal. This mode has analogies and antecedents, and so a look at depictions of vices in other art forms, and in the sermons and theology of the time, is helpful.

Two main sources for the morality form and allegorical method have been identified, the most important and best known being the *Psychomachia* of Prudentius, the fourth-century Spanish Christian poet. This poem presents an epic battle with individual and group combats, between the Seven Deadly Sins and the Seven Cardinal Virtues (with man's soul as the battlefield, allegorically speaking). While this poem was doubtless of great influence in the Middle Ages, it is also true that it is a distant and probably indirect source for the morality plot.[6] From the *Psychomachia* comes a conception of the sins as grotesque and unalterably opposed to the virtues: they are seen as they exist, not as they can disguise themselves. Systematic theological investigation thus depicted them, and as well dwelt upon the relationships between sins as being fixed in sequences, whereby one sin leads to another (the image of a tree, with a trunk and branches, is prevalent).[7] The second source is iconographical: depictions of the sins in sculpture, stained glass, painting and manuscript illumination have been studied to trace traditions of portrayal. The importance of such artifacts in instructing the illiterate faithful was great. As Adolph Katzenellenbogen has shown, the artists tried to suggest the energy and threat of evil through static depiction.[8] The result is vividly grotesque portrayals of deformity and torment which horrify the viewer by showing him the results of sin. Both literary and artistic depictions showed forth the horrible essence of evil as a warning to the faithful: sin's opera-

---

6. Potter, "The Idea of a Morality Play," p. 240. Fo ran older view cf. E. N. S. Thompson, *The English Moral Plays* (New Haven, Conn., 1910), pp. 320–33, who traces the influence of the *Psychomachia* and concludes that Prudentius established "the idea upon which all these plays are based."
7. Morton W. Bloomfield, *The Seven Deadly Sins* (East Lansing, Michigan, 1950) has outlined the concept of such structures of the sins admirably, and Chaucer's *Parson's Tale* provides a contemporary treatment.
8. *Allegories of the Vices and Virtues in Medieval Art* (London, 1939; New York, 1965), pp. 58 ff.

tion and effects are seen directly, and there is little attention to deceit.

These sources do not tell the whole story, and their importance for the morality plays has been perhaps overestimated while other artistic and theological ideas have been relatively overlooked. In non-dramatic writings, other ideas than battle, siege or assault on a castle are used to suggest how sin operates. Most important, since we find it used repeatedly in the plays, is the notion of the human journey as a quest or pilgrimage to the Holy City, during which the Seven Deadly Sins waylay the pilgrim. In the *Pélerinage de la Vie Humaine* (c. 1355), to touch upon only one example, the pilgrim is a just and incorruptible man, and the sins are depicted as foul hags who (except Wrath) assault him directly. The sins are seen by us exactly as they appear to the hero – an idea which is used again in the morality. The basic innovation is the introduction as a character of a mankind figure, as happens in every morality (except possibly *Hickscorner*), and as a result the sins act upon man, not within him (as in the *Psychomachia*). Man becomes either the object of attempts at enslavement or capture, as in the *Pélerinage* and *The Faerie Queene*, or of (more usually) blandishments, arguments and temptations to stray.

One could speculate that the introduction of man and the consequent development away from the battle motif stemmed from a desire for greater variety and subtlety in the plays – at least, such seem to have been the results. The first important scene from which a play's action develops is usually the encounter of the hero with vices who seduce him, so the first focus mingles theology and psychology: why does man sin? If man knows sin to be ultimately damning, how can it operate upon him? The motives of the vices are easy to see, being part of the allegory, but man's motives must be clear, just as the theological question of what constitutes a sin is important. An action? A thought? A lusting?

The opposition of flesh and spirit, whereby our soul is seen as imprisoned within "that stinking dunghill" (*Mankind*, l. 204), located our proclivity to sin in the flesh and tended to see the soul as in itself relatively free of promptings to sin. Chaucer's Parson linked our readiness to sin to the fall – a traditional idea:

There may ye seen that deedly synne hath, first, suggestion of the feend, as sheweth heere by the naddre; and afterward, the delit of the flessh, as sheweth heere by Eve; and after that, the consentynge of resoun, as sheweth heere by Adam. (l. 330)

The degree of man's corruption as a result of the fall was a crucial question – indeed, perhaps *the* crucial question – in the theological disputes over justification in the fifteenth and sixteenth centuries. Concupiscence, resulting from original sin, prompts us to sin even after our baptism,[9] but the extent of its power was debated. Chaucer's Parson gives an account of the process of sinning, beginning in fleshly concupiscence and proceeding through delight:

> Now shall ye understonde in what manere that synne wexeth or encreeseth in man. The firste thyng is thilke norrisynge of synne of which I spak biforn, thilke fleshly concupiscence./ And after that comth the subjeccioun of the devel, this is to seyn, the develes bely, with which he bloweth in man the fir of flesshly concupiscence. And after that, a man bethynketh him wheither he wol doon, or no, thilke thing to which he is tempted./ And thanne, if that a man withstonde and weyve the firste entisynge of his flessh and of the feend, thanne is it no synne; and if it so be that he do nat so, thanne feeleth he anoon a flambe of delit./ And thanne is it good to be war, and kepen him wel, or elles he wol falle anon into consentynge of synne; and thanne wol he do it, if he may have tyme and place. (ll. 349 ff.)

The notion of attraction is strong here. Natural desires to sin (concupiscence) are awakened within man to do the devil's work of assaulting the reason. Concupiscence, the *fomes peccati* or "tinder of sin," needed only the spark of attraction to set it aflame although, as the Parson makes clear, the reason is still naturally able to choose between sin and righteousness. This view, developed through the fifteenth century, holds that when the pilgrim has done the best that he can (*facere quod in se est*) by using his unimpaired natural reason to resist temptation, God is committed to infuse grace to adorn his good works.[10] The importance of subjective rationality is notable. Later, in the Reformation, Luther and especially Calvin were to attack this view, and revert to a

9. David C. Steinmetz, *Misericordia Dei: The Theology of Johannes von Staupitz in its Late Medieval Setting* (Leiden, 1968), p. 113. Cf. E. Jane Dempsey-Douglass, *Justification in Late Medieval Preaching: A Study of John Geiler* (Leiden, 1966), p. 110.
10. Heiko Oberman, *Harvest of Late Medieval Theology: Gabriel Biel and Late Medieval Nominalism* (Harvard, 1963), pp. 146–77. As Oberman concludes, "Biel's doctrine of justification is essentially Pelagian" (p. 177).

more Augustinian position of man's *total* depravity after the fall, and his total dependence upon God's grace. As Calvin said, man should "utterly forsake confidence in his own virtue, and hold that all his strength rests in God alone."[11] In this paper, however, I am concerned mainly with the early period of the morality play's development (c. 1480–1540), the time when Vice was becoming prominent. At this stage man seems generally to have been thought of as balanced between right reason and corrupt concupiscence, rather than as being totally depraved.[12]

The Christian pilgrim must also necessarily undergo temptation so that he may know if he has God's love in his heart. Every temptation overcome is a victory over the devil, and so "lead us not into temptation" seems generally to have been taken as a prayer that those temptations which we cannot withstand may be kept from us.[13] "The life of man on earth is a warfare" (Job 7:1) was a favourite text to describe the necessary warfare with temptation.

Before looking at the dramatic implications of these theological insights into temptation, we can briefly note some ramifications of the concept of the Seven Deadly Sins. First, as Bloomfield notes, confessions of the sins (wherein they are given speaking parts) become prevalent; and this is developed in Langland's *Piers Plowman* where the sins, considerably personalized, show in their confessions that they have mastered all persons and classes.[14] Langland includes considerable humour here, for example with the confession of Gluttony whose easy turn from intended confession when he passes by the ale-house anticipates Falstaff's frequent vows of future repentance. Second, tracing too direct a course from the *Psychomachia* to the plays obscures the fact that the concept of the Seven Deadly Sins had more or less run its course

11. *Institutes of the Christian Religion*, ed. J. T. McNeill, Library of Christian Classics (Philadelphia, 1960), II, ii, 9.
12. As David Bevington has noted, in *From "Mankind" to Marlowe* (Cambridge, Mass., 1962), p. 152, later interludes present us with casts of elect and hopelessly unregenerate characters who pursue their separate courses. These plays have dispensed with the notion of temptation almost entirely, and present their sinners as self-seduced and evil.
13. Hugh Latimer, *Sermons*, Parker Society (London, 1854), p. 437 [Seventh sermon on the Lord's Prayer], and *Middle English Sermons*, ed. W. O. Ross, EETS, Orig. Series, No. 209 (London, 1938), pp. 11 ff. [Sermon 2].
14. Bloomfield, *The Seven Deadly Sins*, pp. 186–200. Cf. *Piers Plowman*, Passus V.

by the fifteenth and sixteenth centuries. Increased stress was coming to be laid upon morally ambiguous situations, and the plausible arguments for sin. This was not new, of course – Gregory had noted in the *Moralia* how faults appear as virtues:

> For cruelty is frequently exercised with punishing sins, and it is counted justice; and immoderate anger is believed to be the meritoriousness of righteous zeal. . . . Frequently negligent remissness is regarded as gentleness and forbearance. . . . When a fault then appears like virtue, we must needs consider that the mind abandons its fault the more slowly, in proportion as it does not blush at what it is doing.[15]

Much later, Thomas Dekker was similarly absorbed by the problem, in *The Bel-man of London* (1608):

> All *Vices* maske themselves with the Vizards of *Vertue*: they borrow their names, the better and more currantly to passe without suspition: for murder will be called *Manhood*, *Drunkenness* is now held to be *Phisicke*, *Impudence* is *Audacitie*, *Riot* good fellowship, &c. So are these *Villaines* (whose faces I meane to discover) painted over with fresh orient colours, because their lookes may be more pleasing and less suspected to have craft underneath them. (E2ᵛ)

The deceitfulness of vice is of course prevalent in the plays, as the vices disguise themselves and otherwise pass themselves off with the externals of virtue. However, Gregory is also looking at the moral ambiguity of given situations, and such ambiguities seem increasingly to have concerned writers. For example, the trial of Lady Meed in *Piers Plowman*, Passus III, contains much in her defence which is convincing, on the surface at least. *A Dispitison Bitwene a God Man and the Devel*, a poem in the Vernon manuscript, proceeds by argument over each of the seven sins in turn, with the Devil being allowed ample space to defend each. After each of his arguments comes the formula, "The gode Mon understod/ That that the tothur seide was not good" (ll. 191–2), and the good man is able to marshal confutations. However, the Devil's arguments are strong, proceeding from the ways of this world, and the poem shows that its author realizes the complexity of the problem of sin.[16] The complex moral questions lead to interiorizing

---

15. *Morals on the Book of Job*, III, 544–6; quoted by Spivack, *Shakespeare and the Allegory of Evil*, p. 156.
16. Bloomfield, *The Seven Deadly Sins*, p. 170.

sin, placing emphasis upon the motives of the doer rather than just the deed. The distinctions mentioned above from Gregory and Dekker are just a few of the subjects investigated in sermons and other confessional literature, and by 1385 there is, in Bloomfield's view, a "generally felt need for a more adequate analysis of sin than that provided by the ordinary classification."[17] As well, as this brief survey has attempted to show, there were various available ways to depict sin. Rather than the motifs of assault and siege provided by the *Psychomachia* tradition, perhaps the morality playwrights present man meeting with plausible, deceptive foes and needing his knowledge, his reason and his innate knowledge of the good to escape deception or self-deception.

Concupiscence, temptation and the attractiveness and plausibility of sin to appear morally ambiguous, are summed up in Shakespeare's phrase, "Fair is foul and foul is fair," and by Macbeth, a man who faces evil's plausibility, its deceit and its ability to induce self-deception. Ambiguity, whereby evil and good become inextricable, runs through this play in which the hero is at once a "dead butcher" and the most continually sympathetic character, while Macduff can on the other hand believe Malcolm capable of whoremongering and avarice, and can yet think these not unfit characteristics for Scotland's future hero-king. Confusion reigns, and "nothing is but what is not." Shakespeare has created another moral Gordian knot in Falstaff (often read now as a fat "reverend Vice") who is able to counter attacks upon himself with plausible arguments, and whose witty deceitfulness is exceeded only by his self-deception. But he remains a problem for theatregoers because his venalities are balanced by his immense warmth and humour: while critics attempt to explain away our reactions to his rejection they do not, I think, explain them. One non-Shakespearian example likewise concerned with moral ambiguity is the Bower of Bliss episode in Book II of *The Faerie Queene*:

> A place pickt out by choice of best alive,
> That natures worke by art can imitate:
> In which what ever in this worldly state
> Is sweet, and pleasing unto living sense,
> Or that may dayntiest fantasie aggrate,
> Was poured forth with plentifull dispence.

17. Ibid., p. 190.

Sir Guyon's destruction of the bower has shocked many readers, who have taken it as wanton iconoclasm. Graham Hough, interestingly, concludes that Spenser's moral position (which necessitates the destruction) collides with his poetic sensibility (which creates the bower so lavishly and beautifully): his description has an independent life which works against his theme because "some things that are poetically important tend to run counter to the morality that is consciously invoked."[18] This is close to saying that Spenser is of the devil's party without knowing it, or to admitting that he has nullified his professed intentions through introducing extraneous elements – which, as we saw earlier, has been charged against the morality playwrights because of their passages of humour and low comedy.

I have introduced these two far greater writers only to suggest that we may find in them moral ambiguities analogous to those confronting us in the vices of the plays, who are at once evil and comic. The moralities are plays of evil; they reflect some of the theological uncertainties of the fifteenth and sixteenth centuries, and in them evil is a real and confusing problem. The evil in the plays has power, is subtle in its shifts, and is plausible and enticing to the mankind-pilgrim who encounters it. The plays attempt to stage a plausible action which investigates not only the *effects* of sin, but also its *operation* in a world tinged with concupiscence.

Man makes the morality plot intensely personal. As he undergoes his conflict, he "stands for us," and hence there is the problem of making his reactions and decisions dramatically convincing, especially his relationships with evil. The usual solution, it seems, was to make the vices comically appealing, so that the hero's amusement (which we share) enables us to understand how he is misled. In John MacQueen's terms, humour supplies the needed "realism" to the allegory, giving a dramatic parallel to the hoped-for delights which tempt the hero to sin.[19] Comedy is the main vice weapon. In play after play the vices emphasize their merriment, as does Naught in *Mankind*:

18. *A Preface to "The Faerie Queene"* (New York, 1962), p. 165.
19. *Allegory* (London, 1973), p. 71. Cf. Thompson, *English Moral Plays*, p. 358, who says, "to dwell too fully on the nature of the temptation . . . introduced a coarse realism that soon submerged the ethical purpose of the play." My own view is opposite – that the nature of the temptation was important, and that it is comedy which makes it real and immediate for us.

> My name is Naught, I love well to make merry;
> I have be sithen with the common tapster of Bury;
> I played so long the fool that I am even very weary. (ll. 266–9)

Similarly, the Vice in *King Darius* tells us:

> Hey, lusty laddes, who can be more merier?
> I thynke inowe can be more soryer
> I lyve at mine own pleasure
> I have every thinge at my owne measure. (D 1)

The vices promise the hero (and us) that fun will ensue, as in *The Four Elements*, where we are reminded of our presence in a hall:

> And I wyll go fet hyther a company,
> That ye shall here them syng as swetly
> As they were angelles clere.
> And yet I shall bryng hydyr a nother sort
> Of lusty bluddes to make dysport
> That shall both daunce and spring
> And torne clene above the ground
> With fryscas and with gambawdes round
> That all the hall shall ryng. (E iii)

They also decry their dour opponents, the virtues, through ridicule, as Sensuality in *I Nature*, for example, routs Reason and Innocency:

> fy. pece no more of thys dysputacyon
> Here be many fantasyes/to dryve forth the day
> That one chatreth lyke a pye/that other lyke a jay. (b i^v)

As an audience, we would probably begin by sharing the hero's virtuous, albeit untried, principles of right living. Following the hero into his seduction we credit the methods of the vices (who always present a better case *dramatically*) and therefore we allow that evil can operate. This perhaps disturbs our moral sensibility, because the great contrast between the vices and the strait-laced virtues affects us, and the vices do appeal to us by making us laugh. Further, the vices succeed at times in detaching us from our moral attitudes and making us relax, momentarily suspending our moral judgments or making us add to our sense that they are evil the further response that they are entertaining and funny. Many critics have sensed this amusement, as I mentioned earlier, but they have been unsure why, and have either called it functionless comic relief or have suspected that the play is faulty. "Relief" it may be, but it is part of the plays' method, which is conflict between virtue and vice. Rather than undertaking with the virtues "as their common purpose, to persuade the audience that it is better being good than bad,"[20] it seems to me that the vices oppose goodness and attempt to attract new adherents through comedy.

As the vices amuse us, we can be said to share the hero's seduction. We have believed in it, have felt the springs of sympathetic laughter, and have perhaps even been called upon to assist in seduction (as in *Mankind*, when we sing the amazingly scatological song and, later, hold our peace when Titivillus asks us to). The play is not, then, attempting at a unified impression, but is rather attempting to touch us vicariously, and pull our emotions in more than one way.

One could object that the vices cannot keep counsel – they'll tell all: that is, through asides they tell us how evil they are, as they seem unable to lie to us. In some plays, such as *Three Lawes*, we are overwhelmed by the amount of such information, but in others it can serve as an infrequent disturbing reminder to us. There is also the question of the tone of such pronouncements. Infidelity, in L. Wager's *Life and Repentance of Mary Magdalene*, is explicit:

> no beware of me Infidelitie,
> Like as Faith is the roote of all goodnesse,
> So am I the head of all iniquitie,
> The well and spring of all wickednesse
> Mary syr, yet I convey my matters cleane,
> Like as I have a visour of vertue. (A 4)

(Notably, however, Pride, Satan and Cupiditie share Infidelity's sense of being "top dog," as their boasting soliloquies elsewhere indicate.) Vices in other plays often seem to speak as if they don't have to lie to us – after all, they can confide in their friends, can't they? For example, Folly in *Mundus et Infans* addresses a proud aside to us:

20. Spivack, *Shakespeare and the Allegory of Evil*, p. 123.

> A ha! Syrs, let the cat wynke.
> For all ye wote not what I thynke,
> I shall drawe hym suche a draught of drynke
> That conscyence he shall awaye cast. (ll. 649–52)

Titivillus in *Mankind* goes even further, to an outright request for applause as he exits:

> Farewell, everychon! For I have done my game,
> For I have brought Mankind to mischief and to shame. (ll. 606–7)

To these direct self-explanations, as to other parts of the vices' performances, a variety of responses seems possible.

One might expect to see the seduced hero, during his life-in-sin, becoming the victim or prisoner of sin; however, the life-in-sin changed very early from a homiletic progression to a comic sequence. Its importance (showing the operation of evil) is attested by its becoming the largest part of many plays, and its concentrated comic effect is the dramatic parallel to the immediate delights and advantages of sin. The church had always taught that we are especially prone to sin at times when its delights may be expected. Surveying his flock on Low Sunday, one preacher ruefully observes that men are already turning from Lenten penitence to summer sinfulness because the weather cooperates with the Devil: "metes and drynkes amenden and been more delicious than they were, and many beth now fayre clothed, and wymmen nycely arayed. All this hym thenketh that is conabull to hym, and thus with many othur colours he disseyvith the pepull."[21] Sadly, it is a long time until next Easter. Similarly in the plays, repentance can apparently be put off until, in Mankind's words, "to-morn or the next day" (*Mankind*, l. 732). All seems innocent, and everyone seems happy. A deepening involvement with evil may be symbolically suggested: the hero may meet new friends, and become involved with a large group of vices, and as well the comedy may become broader, more nonsensical, and more venal. Both expedients have the theatrical function of enhancing the vices and making them more active entertainers for the hero's (and our) benefit.

That our attitudes as an audience are important is attested by

21. *Middle English Sermons*, p. 133 [Sermon 23].

the number of opportunities given to the vices, in play after play, to approach us directly, especially when the hero is absent. Direct revelation and the arousal of laughter result. One remarkable example is the vice-conspiracy in *Mankind*, which begins with Mischief nonsensically playing a quack doctor (an idea borrowed from the mumming plays), proceeds through the gathering of admission-money to see Titivillus, and ends with the cheating of the devil. The convention of the vice introducing himself to us in a comic soliloquy became established, and some of these opportunities became "turns" of comical nonsense – for example, Idleness in *Wit and Wisdom*:

> A sirra my masters how fare you at this blessed day
> what I wen all this company are come to se a play
> what lokest the goodfellow didest the nere
> se man before
> here is a gasing I am the best man in
> the compony when there is no more
> as for my properties I am sure you
> knowe them of old
> I can Eate tell I sweate & work
> tell I am a cold. (ll. 178–87)

The allegorical "properties" established are vestigial and comically paradoxical, while Idleness's main point seems to be his self-praise for his gifts at comic soliloquizing. The nonsense of this late, comic, example is only a development of tendencies apparent in earlier plays. As mentioned earlier, Bale's *Three Lawes* is nearly humourless, but Bale apparently feels constrained to introduce his chief vice, Infidelity, in the conventional way – here with a street cry like Nichol Newfangle's in *Like Will to Like*:

> Brom, brom, brom, brom, brom. Bye brom bye
> bye. Bromes for shoes and pouchringes, Botes and
> buskyns for newe bromes. Brom, brom, brom.
> Marry God geve ye good even.
> And the holy man saynt Steven,
> Sende ye a good newe yeare.
> I wolde have brought ye the paxe
> Or els an ymage of waxe.
> If I had knowne ye heare. (A 6)

Being allowed to work directly upon our sympathies, the Vice characters evolve a new attitude to, or consciousness of, the audience *as* an audience at play to be "amused and flattered, diverted and entertained."[22] This contrasts with the virtues' conception of us as a "congregation" to be edified. Remembering the nature of the conflict in the plays, we need not worry that the vices never get us "involved in the moral judgment of the play"[23] – why should the vices seek a moral judgment? They realize (and remind us) that we are "come to se a play," and they forge, through laughter, a group of individual spectators into an audience. Hence they remind us of the communal nature of the theatre, and show that they realize their function as entertainers. In *The Four Elements*, the hero is chided

> For all the folyshe arguynge that thou hast had
> With that knave experiens, that hath made
> All these folke therof wery,
> For all they that be nowe in this hall,
> They be the most part my servauntes all,
> And love pryncypally
> Disports as dauncynge syngynge
> Toys tryfuls laughynge gestynge
> For connynge they set not by. (E 4)

An important aspect of our humanity gains expression through these vices – the sense of society, diversion and innocent merriment which found expression in the period in folk games and plays, church-ales, May games and dances and singing. Many such diversions are presented by vices and although some are undoubtedly scurrilous in the extreme, not all are, and it is only the extremely pietistic virtues who find fault with them all when encountered. Our sense of theatre is reinforced, in play after play, by the vices' use of conventional stage business, such as the vice-greeting, the comic proclamation, fights, and so on. We might add (on the evidence of *Three Lawes*) the convention that the vices are funny. Like the appearance of Charlie Chaplin dressed as the "little fellow," these conventions arouse our expectations of familiar entertainment.

22. Anne Righter, *Shakespeare and the Idea of the Play* (Harmondsworth, Middlesex, 1967), p. 30.
23. Ibid., p. 32.

To sum up, the use of comedy to suggest the operation of evil in the plays does not lead us to condemn comedy *per se*: rather it is the weapon the vices use to seduce the hero and disarm us. We are faced with a situation of some complexity, since we must simultaneously account for our moral attitudes (bolstered by the virtues), our knowledge of vice names and plans, a lurking feeling that all will turn out badly, and, on the other hand, our laughter at the vices, many of whose actions are apparently harmless. A spectrum of attitude is possible to us, as we are pulled two ways. The resolution of this situation, it seems to me, lies in the fortunes of the hero, both in this world and beyond it. If a morality play were to end with the hero happy, prosperous and reprobate (if, for example, *Mankind* ended with the exit of the merry crew to play football), then we would be eminently justified in calling it an *immorality* play and perhaps, upon reflection, feeling outraged. But morality plots proceed from the life-in-sin (illusory prosperity) to the phase of retribution or death, and here occurs the dramatization of evil's effects. The vices may assert their mastery over their victim (as in *Mankind*, where they nearly bring him to suicide), or they may rob or desert their victim. The pilgrim-hero undergoes suffering which often leads to despair, and his eyes are finally opened to the superficially attractive companions with whom he has consorted. We, who have known in the backs of our minds all along that something like this would happen (just as we know Falstaff's fate), suffer the reassertion of our full moral censors as we hear about the evil aspects of the apparent fun we have witnessed. Morality usually reasserts itself with shocking swiftness, as in the Digby *Mary Magdalene*:

> woman, woman, why art thou so on-stabyll?
> ful bytterly thys blysse it wol be bowth;
> why art thou a-yens god so veryabyll?
> wy thynkes thou nat god made the of nowth?
> In syn and sorow thou art browth,
> fleschly lust is to ye full delectabyll;
> salve for thi sowle must be sowth,
> and leve the werkes wayn and veryabyll. (ll. 588 ff.)

Similarly in *Mankind*, Mercy's entrance with a "baleis" (whip), the flight of the vices and Mankind's plight as he lies on the ground in despair provide an impressive tableau of eventual ruin.

Thus far we have seen how humour became a vice-weapon, creating one side of the contrast in the plays, and how the vice-group tended to receive more emphasis as humorous opportunities in the plays were developed. Routines and conventional humorous business also became more prominent. As well as an opportunity, this comic playing presented a challenge to the troupes, and I wish next to look at this in connection with the Vice character. Between 1480 and 1540 or so, one notices a development between plays such as *Mankind* and *Johan the Evangelist* (in which the vices are a relatively undifferentiated group), and later plays in which the vices have achieved cohesiveness and organization. One player has prominence, is very adept at humour, and is the Vice. It seems to me that there are four reasons for these developments, first of which is that cast-reduction and the adoption of the pilgrim-seduction type of plot resulted in the necessity (and possibility) of there being only single vices or small groups to effect the seduction.[24] Secondly, the didacticism of the plays, it appears, necessitated that the seducer "should be conspicuous as the *root* of all the evils represented."[25] This does not mean that every play presented the concept of the Seven Deadly Sins, nor that the sequence of sins in every play began with Pride or Avarice (traditionally, each was the "root of all evil"). This concept was falling into disuse. Equally, the seducer is not in every play the most serious sin in the group. In *Magnyfycence* Fancy, or capricious self-indulgence, leads to the four court-vices who are Skelton's chief objects of attack. In Medwall's *Nature*, Sensuality leads the hero to Pride, who admits at one point that the Deadly Sins can only act upon an already corrupted hero.[26] The plays show "the sequence by which one moral evil, having established itself in the human heart, makes a path for the next,"[27] but only in the sense that any sin provides a place to start, and that sin will pluck on sin. Finally, the custom grew in the sixteenth century of giving the chief Vice a generic name, such as "the formal Vice, Iniquity,"[28]

24. Bevington, *From "Mankind" to Marlowe*, pp. 114–15, considers cast-reduction by the professional troupes, while Spivack (pp. 151–4), emphasizes the intimacy necessary to the seduction plot.
25. Spivack, *Shakespeare and the Allegory of Evil*, p. 138.
26. *II Nature*, sig. f i^v. In contrast, *Youth* presents a plot wherein Pride leads to Lechery, and the Digby *Mary Magdalene* shows how Lechery leads to Pride.
27. Spivack, *Shakespeare and the Allegory of Evil*, p. 142.
28. *Richard III*, III, i, 82.

Sin, Infidelity, Nature, Courage, Inclination, and so on. Remarkably, some of the names are morally neutral in quality.

Turning to the third reason, the idea of moral sequence does not establish why, for a given hero, a particular Vice should be selected as tempter – and that this choice is not capricious is shown by the selection scenes which exist in some plays. It seems that special *attractiveness* to the hero, or suitability to his temperament, profession or situation in life often dictated the choice of a tempter, such a one as would have the best chance of success, as the Flesh tells Lechery in the Digby *Mary Magdalene*:

> now, the lady lechery, yow must don your attendans,
> for yow be flower fayrest of femynyte;
> yow xal go desyyr servyse, and byn at hur atendauns,
> for ye xal sonest enter ye beral of bewte. (ll. 422–5)

Attacking a man at his weakest point is the *modus operandi* of evil, as is vividly portrayed in a contemporary sermon:

> Seynt Gregore, telleth in a boke that he made that the dewell is evermore aspyinge uppon a man to what synne that he is most inclynynge to, and to that synne he will evermore nyght and day tempte him ther-to. For the dewell . . . has the condicions of a theffe. For what tyme that a theffe will breke an hous or a wall, where the howse is febulleste and the wall lowest, ther will he sonest breke in. And so fareth the dewell. For to that synne that a man geues hym moste to, to that synne shall the dewell tempte hym moste to
>
> .   .   .   .
>
> For first when that he commeth to tempte a man to synne, he will begynne with smale synnes and veniall. And yiff a man consent ther-to, than he will tempte hem with gretter synnes.[29]

In this we see a rationale for some plays' beginning with minor pecadilloes, and leading to greater sins, and also for the apparent harmlessness with which heroes may begin to sin. As well, the sin with which a man begins is psychologically revealing of the way the particular man falls, rather than revealing how *sin* always begins. Remembering that the dramatic metaphor for attraction and desire is humour, it is natural to find the first seducer normally

29. *Middle English Sermons*, p. 218 [Sermon 38]. Cf. Gregory, *Moralia*, XIV, 213.

being given a preponderance of the comedy. Comic acting, then, is important for the plays as wholes – the virtues can seem prim and stiff, and man little more than frail, but the vices (and especially the seducer) must brim with arresting energy. Badly told jokes and wooden lines won't do because the seduction would seem unbelievable, the audience would be bored rather than amused, and all would be marred.

Theatrically, the corollary of this is the importance of good comic actors for the morality troupes. One may assume that in a troupe containing men of varying talents, the role of chiefly pleasing initial seducer would fall to the best comedian – and the better he was, the better for them. It is also true that good comedians are (and probably were) very rare, since comedy is a difficult art requiring talent, endless practice and polish, as one memorable clown from our own century has said:

> The public has a rooted idea that all you have to do in order to become a clown is to practise a whole week long every morning in front of the glass, rolling your eyes and putting out your tongue . . . but a long tongue and a big mouth no more go to complete a clown than a paint-brush does an artist or horn-rimmed spectacles a poet. No clown can be a real clown without the help of tradition and method, and an exhaustive technical training.
>
> Your clown, just as much as any other artist, is the product of tradition. . . .[30]

The need for good comedians doubtless became greater as comic conventions developed, such as improvization or "gagging":

> *Here the vyce shal turne the proclamation to some contrary sence everie time all for money hath read it, and here followeth the proclamation. (All for Money, l. 1008)*

What a poor comic would do with that, one shudders to think. In connection with this last point one recalls that broad comedy increases vastly with the appearance of the Vice, and is always more prevalent in plays for professional troupes.[31] Having developed a plot requiring comedy, playwrights tried, I think, to facilitate it by

30. Grock [pseud. Charles A. Wettach] *Life's a Lark* (London, 1931), pp. 225–6.
31. Bevington, *From "Mankind" to Marlowe*, Ch. II.

not dissipating the talents of the comedian. They tended more and more to type-cast him, producing an amalgam of the appeals for sympathy, the comic sequences, the histrionics and deceit, the talent to delight and seduce, and so on, into one undoubled part. The other actors were required to double a variety of roles and to act in a more formal style.

The fourth pressure to develop the Vice arises from the exigencies of cast reduction and doubling, an area pioneered and mapped by Professor Bevington. The growing emphasis upon vices in plays for small troupes led to the problem of how to organize doubling coherently, especially when the dramatist wished to allow vice-action independent of the mankind hero (whose presence had hitherto always provided a ready motive for entrances, and who was available to fill the time during costume-changes). Some other motive and central character was needed, and the motive of the vices seeking out their chief or entering at his bidding was used. *Lusty Juventus* (1550) will illustrate. Elaboration of one more vice role than there are actors available necessitates a suppression which is organized around Hypocrisy, at the beginning of the stage of vice action. I refer to the dialogue between Satan and his son Hypocrisy, during which they resolve upon no course of action – Hypocrisy rather promises to do something and cheers his father up. The main dramatic points are the complaints over the progress of the Reformation and the boasts of Hypocrisy over his "doings" – which allow the author to lampoon alleged Catholic superstitions:

> Holy skinnes, holy bulles,
> Holy Rochettes and coules:
> Holy crouches and staves:
> Holy hoodes holy cappes:
> Holy Miters holy hattes:
> A good holy holy knaves. (ll. 421 ff.)

There is also a deal of broad buffoonery between the pair, especially the depiction of Satan as an ingenuous bumpkin. The religious polemic is incidental to the plot, but it functions as anti-Catholic satire and as characterization of Hypocrisy. Structurally, Satan opens the episode with a monologue, and at its completion he leaves the stage to Hypocrisy (l. 492), and this vice remains behind to gloat, to plan and to await his victim. Hence Juventus seems doomed before he appears, and it would be fair to say that the whole vice episode is Hypocrisy's scene since he remains dramatically central. As he is the first seducer the other vices naturally look to him as leader, and that he alone has conversed with Satan gives him dramatic emphasis. His "Vice-hood" is apparent from the organization of the forces of evil around him, and by the way Juventus is attracted to hypocrisy as an excuse for his backsliding. It is not just asserted that Hypocrisy is chief, but also effectively dramatized, and it is interesting in this connection that in the probable doubling requirements (as worked out by Professor Bevington), both Juventus and Hypocrisy have undoubled parts.[32]

Although still undoubled, and of theoretically equal weight, Juventus's part seems comparatively less fat, as he is removed from the action for a lengthy period. The morality play becomes thoroughly a play of Vice when the next step is taken – when the Vice is undoubled but the mankind hero is duplicated, so that the Vice in effect meets a *series* of victims. While this occurs mainly after 1550, I should like in closing to look briefly at Bale's *Three Lawes* (*c.* 1538) wherein it is anticipated. This miracle-morality play is structured upon the historical idea of the three successive covenants of God: Nature, Moses (Old Testament Law) and Christ (New Testament Gospel, and Protestant Christianity). Being successive and separate, these dispensations must be overthrown one after the other, to show how the two earlier laws remained abrogated until finally restored by the triumph of Christ (and Protestantism). There is also a succession of vices, since each covenant is attacked by appropriate opponents. Bale needed some structural principle to bind this all together so that it would not appear to be three separate playlets. As well, some character was needed to whom the other vices could have easy recourse and conversation, so that their natures (especially their likeness to Catholics) could be emphasized. If the play had been presented as a massive outdoor morality, separate *sedes* could have been provided and simultaneous staging accomplished, but the limitation to five actors denies this possibility. Instead, Bale created Infidelity to head the "six vyces, or frutes of Infydelyte," as the casting-list depicts them. The homiletic point, that all attacks upon true religion proceed from faithlessness, is clear, and the polemic point that Infidelity is Catholic is shown by such means as the

32. Ibid., p. 145.

opening reference to saints and "the paxe" in Infidelity's greeting which I quoted earlier. Dramatically, Infidelity is chief because he solves Bale's organizational problem by providing a link between episodes, and an ear to whom the specific vices can reveal their evil exploits. He does not participate directly in any overthrow and, as I have mentioned, is depicted at a few places as comic (albeit feebly, as if Bale knew he had a convention to satisfy). Structurally, Infidelity has virtually no doubling and hence the longest part, and is called upon to deliver numerous soliloquies covering pauses in the action during costume-changes. Only the failure of evil and restoration of Christ (i.e., the Reformation) drives him from sight.

The difference between Bale's humourless diatribe and the amusing unregeneracy and social satire of such plays as *Like Will to Like* or *All for Money* is one of tone, not structure, since these plays are likewise centred upon an undoubled Vice who meets successive groups of mankind-victims (with occasional brief contrasting episodes of virtuous men and their companions). This paper has tried to show how the morality plays concern themselves with evil, including comedy within them as characterization of some aspects of that evil. Further, some of the changes and challenges which comic playing brought to the genre exerted, as we have seen, an influence upon the development of the Vice and his role.

The Reconstruction of Stage Action from Early Dramatic Texts

T. W. CRAIK

"A play read affects the mind like a play acted." Dr. Johnson's remark has the weight of his good sense behind it. A reader will grasp the essentials of a play as surely as a spectator will: theme, plot, character, mood, will be equally clear to both. Yet unless the reader is experienced in the ways of the theatre, he will hardly be able to reconstruct the full effect which the scene he is reading would make in performance. This is a fact more widely recognized in our own century than in Dr. Johnson's, and its recognition has produced some excellent criticism of plays, notably that of Harley Granville Barker, whose general and particular insights were matched at every point by his awareness of what could be done, and how it could be done, on a stage – especially the stage of the Elizabethan public theatre. Most of us no longer see that stage precisely as Granville Barker and his contemporaries saw it; most of us, indeed, are resigned to never establishing its ultimate details. But I hope most of us agree that Granville Barker's approach, conspicuous for imagination united with commonsense, was a valuable influence on Shakespearean criticism and production.

One of his methods was to invoke the evidence of the original texts and their original stage directions. This method of reconstructing stage action is the subject of my paper, in which I shall examine some incidents from well-known plays by dramatists contemporary with the young Shakespeare. I shall try to suggest some of the different kinds of evidence that we may usefully take into account when trying to discover what actually happened when the lines (which are often all we have) were being spoken. Some of the matters I shall be discussing are the relationship of a passage to its source, its resemblance to incidents in contemporary plays, the question of self-consistency within a given play, the implications as to stage properties and the stage itself, and the possibility of interpolation and other corruptions of the text. And since (to anticipate) one of my suggestions will be that we ought to take these things into simultaneous consideration, deciding in each particular instance how much weight we give to one kind of evidence and how much to another, I shall construct the paper not around principles but around passages, and let the principles emerge in their own time as we proceed.

The first passage concerns the killing of Absalon by Joab in Peele's *David and Bethsabe*. It is clear, from this scene and others, that Peele was composing with an open Bible before him, for he accurately versifies Joab's dialogue with the soldier who reports Absalon's entanglement in the oak. The biblical account continues (II Samuel xviii. 14):

> Then said Joab, I wil not thus tarie with thee. And hee tooke three darts in his hande, and thrust them through Absalom, while he was yet alive in the middes of the oke.[1]

"I must not now stand trifling here with thee," says Peele's Joab to the soldier, and he proceeds to hold dialogue with Absalon for some forty lines. Absalon begs Joab to pity him, but Joab refuses, concluding with

> But preach I to thee, while I should revenge
> Thy cursed sinne that staineth Israel,
> And makes her fields blush with her childrens bloud?
> Take that as part of thy deserved plague,
> Which worthily no torment can inflict.
> Abs.　O Joab, Joab, cruell ruthlesse Joab,
> Herewith thou woundst thy Kingly soveraignes heart,
> Whose heavenly temper hates his childrens bloud,
> And will be sicke I know for Absalon.
> O my deere father, that thy melting eyes

1. Christopher Barker's quarto, London, 1583.

77

> Might pierce this thicket to behold thy sonne,
> Thy deerest sonne gor'de with a mortall dart:
> Yet Joab pittie me, pittie my father, Joab,
> Pittie his soules distresse that mournes my life,
> And will be dead I know to heare my death.
> *Joab.* If he were so remorsefull of thy state,
> Why sent he me against thee with the sword?
> All Joab meanes to pleasure thee withall,
> Is to dispatch thee quickly of thy paine.
> Hold Absalon, Joabs pittie is in this,
> In this prowd Absalon is Joabs love.
> *He goes out.*

(ll. 1524–44)

There are no further directions in the Quarto. Dyce (1861) supplies, at the respective ends of Joab's two speeches, "Stabs him" and "Stabs him again; and then exit with Soldier." The Soldier's exit need not concern us, though I am sure Joab's line to him is a dismissal which leaves the two principal characters alone on stage. What I should like to stress is the means of stabbing. Peele's most recent editor (Elmer M. Blistein) annotates Joab's "Take that" with "At this point Joab undoubtedly stabs Absalon with dagger or sword."[2] This is perhaps what he does in the theatre, but if so, he does it because Peele has set the actor a problem. Peele has the three darts in mind, for he has written all three of them into the lines:

> Take *that* as part of thy deserved plague,

and

> Hold Absalon, Joabs pittie is in *this*,
> In *this* prowd Absalon is Joabs love.

Joab has been sent against Absalon "with the sword" in a figurative sense only: Absalon is "gor'de with a mortall dart." The directions we must supply, therefore, in order to be faithful to Peele's intentions, are "Pierces him with a dart" and "Pierces him with two more darts, and exit." Perhaps it could be done convincingly by the Elizabethans, perhaps not. Compare the carefree and probably authorial direction at the beginning of the scene:

> *The battell, and Absalon hangs by the haire.*

2. *The Life and Works of George Peele*, general editor C. T. Prouty, Vol. 3 (New Haven, 1970), p. 276.

"Pd for poleyes [pulleys] & worckmanshipp for to hange absolome, xiiij^d," says Henslowe's *Diary*,[3] possibly referring to this play, possibly to some other play on the same subject. Peele, I am pretty sure, felt that his responsibility ended with the script, and that pulleys and workmanship and darts were the performers' business. Certainly there is nothing in the text to show how this tree is to be represented or how Absalon entangles himself in it (the Bible says he was riding beneath it on his mule); perhaps he is to be "discovered" already suspended. I dwell on the matter in order to remind you how little help we often get from the text in discovering the mechanics of Elizabethan production.[4] The storming of Rabbah, early in the same play, is a case in point. It is modelled on Tamburlaine's storming of Babylon. Joab exchanges defiance with the Ammonites "upon the wals," after which he commands his followers

> Assault ye valiant men of Davids host,
> And beat these railing dastards from their dores.
>
> *Assault, and they win the Tower, and Joab speakes above.*
>
> Thus have we won the Tower, which we will keepe,
> Maugre the sonnes of Ammon, and of Syria.
>
> *Enter Cusay beneath.*
>
> Cusay. Where is lord Joab leader of the host?
>
> Joab. Here is lord Joab leader of the host.
> Cusay come up, for we have won the hold.
>
> *He comes.*
>
> Cusay. In happie hower then is Cusay come. (ll. 211–18)

Cusay has come to recall Urias to David's presence. Joab says, "Here take him with thee then, and goe in peace," and they presently make their farewells with an *Exeunt*. Then Joab's captain Abisay says to him

3. *Henslowe's Diary*, ed. W. W. Greg. Vol. 2 (London, 1908), p. 232.
4. Even when the directions seem clear, as in *Cambises*, l. 464: "Flea him with a false skin." It is unlikely that the actor was wearing a false skin under his robes: it would be a lengthy and indeed an indecent process to strip him of them and of it. More probably the actors had a false skin ready to produce, perhaps throwing a sheet over the body.

> Let us descend, and ope the pallace gate,
> Taking our souldiors in to keepe the hold. (ll. 241–2)

Joab agrees, and another *Exeunt* ends the scene. The general action here is clear and practical. The capture of Babylon (*2 Tamb.* V.i) contains the direction *Alarme, and they scale the walles*, and here Joab leads a scaling party against defenders "above," while the remainder of the stage army is still on the platform at the scene's end and makes its exit on that level. The doubtful questions are whether Urias climbs with Joab and whether Cusay later climbs in his turn. W. J. Lawrence thought a visible staircase might be used both for the assault and for Cusay's ascent (*Pre-Restoration Stage Studies*, p. 37): Blistein (p. 261) regards his idea with justifiable doubt, but he does think Cusay climbs up there somehow. I am not sure even of this. If Cusay ascends now by scaling ladder, he will have to descend again within twenty lines, and Urias with him, so that they can depart in the direction from which Cusay arrived, and this rapid coming and going may look awkward. On the other hand, one would not expect Urias to have hung back when there was fighting to be done: it was in fact his suggestion that they "assault and scale this kingly Tower." I therefore suppose him to be aloft with Joab when Cusay enters. He can then climb down, after "Here take him with thee then, and goe in peace," while Joab speaks nine further lines to Cusay, telling him to urge David to complete the capture of Rabbah himself and thereby gain the glory of the campaign. To complicate matters further, this is not the first time Cusay has been invited to "come up": "Cusay, come up and serve thy lord the King" (l. 72), says David in the opening scene after soliloquizing on Bethsabe's beauty. *Enter Cusay* is the direction at this point, and, after David has given him instructions, *Exit Cusay to Bethsabe*. Then, following seven more lines of soliloquy from the king, comes the further direction, *Cusay to Bethsabe, she starting as something afright*. This does not look like the use of a visible staircase, and Cusay appears to be offstage when first summoned; but at least his conversation with David takes place above, for when Bethsabe is bathing, David *sits above vewing her*. However, it seems to me still an open question whether Joab's "Cusay come up" is any more than an invitation to approach the walls. I have not appealed to the biblical source because it can give us no help here: it is Peele's own idea to combine Cusay's recall of Urias with Joab's taking of Rabbah. Hence we are thrown upon conjecture, just as we are in the final act of *The Spanish Tragedy* (a play without a known source). When Hieronimo says to Castile,

> Let me intreat your grace,
> That when the traine are past into the gallerie,
> You would vouchsafe to throwe me downe the key, (IV. iii. 11–13)

his lines imply that the stage audience will be above. If it were to be on the platform with the performers of Hieronimo's play, there is no reason why the key should not be handed to him, and so Philip Edwards' explanation[5] that Hieronimo is asking Castile to throw it on the floor is as strained as the gesture would be rude; nobody behaves like that except Malvolio returning Olivia's ring to Viola. This is not, of course, to deny that Kyd's mind may have changed in the course of composition, or that the act may have been rewritten by himself or another with new staging in view. The key, in fact, never is thrown down (in any sense of the phrase), but I am not sure that we can therefore infer that rewriting has occurred: Hieronimo's speech in itself may serve Kyd to make his dramatic point, that the royal spectators are hereafter to be considered as locked in the gallery.

Whenever there is evidence of rewriting it may enormously complicate the reconstruction of staging; and, conversely, inconsistent staging provides strong evidence of rewriting. I view with the utmost suspicion any dialogue or direction that seems to call for an upper acting area in *Doctor Faustus*. For example, where the 1604 quarto simply says *Enter Faustus to conjure* (1.234), that of 1616 substitutes *Thunder. Enter Lucifer and 4 devils, Faustus to them with this speech.*[6] There is no warrant in the source for these devils presiding over the scene, and no dramatic merit in it: on the contrary, the ineptitude is astonishing, for the spectators' attention is distracted from Faustus, their shock at Mephostophilis' arrival as a devil is nullified and (worst of all) Lucifer's own dramatic entry in a later scene is forestalled by prematurely bring-

---

5. T. Kyd, *The Spanish Tragedy*, ed. P. Edwards (The Revels Plays, London, 1959), p. 110. Line-references are to this edition, text (with normalized i/j, u/v) from the Scolar Press facsimile of Q1592 (Leeds, 1966).
6. Quotations from Marlowe's plays are from *The Works of Christopher Marlowe*, ed. C. F. Tucker Brooke (Oxford, 1910), normalizing i/j and u/v.

ing him on unheralded, unidentified, and without anything to do. Throughout the scene, moreover, Lucifer is assumed to be at home in hell, whither Faustus sends Mephostophilis to propose terms: his stage presence is therefore at variance with this assumption – not ironically but just senselessly at variance with it. Similarly, in the last act, Faustus' terrifying apprehension – "Looke sirs, comes he not? comes he not?" – is at variance with the premature arrival of Lucifer, Belzebub and Mephostophilis, "To marke him how he doth demeane himself."[7]

A play which has often been suspected of being altered by other hands than the author's is *The Jew of Malta*, though the suspicion has usually been based on a prejudiced view of how the plot ought to develop and how the central character ought to be presented. But I should like to consider the possibility that one line at least has been interpolated, because its presence raises a substantial difficulty in performance. This is when Friar Barnardine has been strangled by Barabas and Ithamore, who then prop up his body as if resting on his staff. Friar Jacomo enters on his way to Barabas, and (since the friars are now rivals in the attempt to convert Barabas and thus secure his money for their separate houses) he thinks Barnardine is standing there to prevent his access. So he addresses him:

7. Greg interprets this diabolical superintendence, like that over the conjuring scene, as an attempt to show Faustus as a puppet in the hands of the infernal powers, and relates it to Mephostophilis' boast (also in this final scene) that he "led [Faustus'] eye" to the scriptural passages which threw him into rebellious despair (*Marlowe's Doctor Faustus, 1604–1616*, Oxford, 1950, pp. 129–132). Related I believe these things are, but I also believe that the prime motive was not to explore Faustus' spiritual position but to exploit spectacle: to give the spectators more devils and shows for their money, and to make use of the neglected upper stage and – with the Good and Evil Angels – the descending throne from the heavens, and possibly a representation of hell-mouth revealed on the inner stage. These passages' stress on spectacle would alone be sufficient to explain their omission from the 1604 quarto, with its austerity of stage demands; and a likely explanation of their tidy and total omission is that they were the recognizable recent additions of a year or two before.

I likewise disagree with Greg's conjecture (p. 132) that these parts of the final scene were written before Faustus' final soliloquy, and that after its composition they were discarded before production. On the contrary, Mephostophilis' lines "his labouring braine/Begets a world of idle fantasies/To over-reach the Divell" seem to me to refer to Faustus' desperate notions of arresting the heavenly bodies, leaping up to his God, being drawn up like a foggy mist, or being changed into water drops.

Bernardine;
Wilt thou not speake? thou think'st I see thee not;
Away, I'de wish thee, and let me goe by:
No, wilt thou not? nay then I'le force my way;
And see, a staffe stands ready for the purpose:
As thou lik'st that, stop me another time.
    Strike him, he fals. Enter Barabas.
    Bar. Why, how now *Iocoma*, what hast thou done?
    Ioco. Why, stricken him that would have stroke at me. (ll. 1677–84)

The difficult line to assimilate into the action is "And see, a staffe stands ready for the purpose." If Jacomo means Barnardine's staff, the line is completely at variance with his fear that Barnardine is waiting to attack him with it. Naturally it raises a laugh in the theatre if Jacomo pulls this staff away and deals a blow to the already falling body of Barnardine, but the laughter is purely at well-timed clownage. In terms of situation and character the action is nonsensical – too nonsensical even for farce. For this reason, when editing the play a few years ago,[8] I felt driven to suggest that Barabas had silently left a second staff on stage so that Jacomo would be tempted to use it. I now wish to withdraw that suggestion, which was my desperate attempt to make sense of the text.[9] My present opinion is that the line may have been interpolated (possibly by Marlowe but more probably by another) on rereading the scene and coming to the final couplet:

> Take in the staffe too, for that must be showne:
> Law wils that each particular be knowne. (ll. 1714–15)

What staff? asked the interpolator, and replied, the one which Jacomo used: therefore I must put it into his hand. Consequently

8. *The New Mermaids* (London, 1966), p. 77.
9. In plays it is usual for a character to say something in explanation of an otherwise unmotivated action he is performing, though there are exceptions, as in *The Changeling* where De Flores hides a sword (with which he will later murder Alonso) in the interval between Acts II and III. Conversely it is also usual for statements to be motivated by action: for example, in *The Jew of Malta*, III. ii. 3 (*The New Mermaids*, London, 1966), I give the line "What, dares the villain write in such base terms?" to Lodowick because it is the dramatic consequence of the direction *Enter Lodow, reading*. Its assignment to Mathias (who has spoken the previous speech) in Q1633 must be an error, and the inference is that a line for Mathias (between this and Lodowick's next line) has been lost. I conjecturally restore it as "Thou villain, durst thou court my Abigail?"

he wrote in the line, forgetting in his confusion that a staff is part of the standard equipment of friars and that Jacomo would have his own, as did Barnardine.

After the problem of the staff in *The Jew of Malta*, consider the problem of the spit in *Edward II*. The difficulty here is that there is a source, which is quite explicit about the details of the murder, and Marlowe's play follows it when Lightborn specifically asks for a fire and a red-hot spit, a table and a feather-bed; but when the murder is actually performed there is provision in the dialogue for the table, on which Matrevis and Gurney are told to stamp, "But not too hard, least that you bruse his body," (l. 2561), but no apparent provision for the spit. From the dialogue one would think that the murder was done with the table and feather-bed alone except for Matrevis' line "I feare mee that this crie will raise the towne," which implies that Edward dies in great pain. Marlowe is especially careful in this play to coordinate action and speech, so the lack of coordination here is surprising. I do not think we can altogether rule out the remote possibility that some of the original dialogue was omitted as being too objectionable to be printed. As the dialogue stands, the technical problem for the actors is con-siderable, because Matrevis and Gurney (who have to be in-structed by Lightborn about how to use the table) receive no further instructions from him, and yet collaborate with him effi-ciently. Sometimes one sees Edward murdered with only part of the equipment, sometimes with all of it.[10] Certainly the combined weight of the source and of Lightborn's earlier requirements is heavy. W. Moelwyn Merchant's suggestion[11] that the murder may have been done behind a curtain I think we must utterly reject. Imagine the baffled fury of Marlowe's audience!

I mentioned, a moment ago, Marlowe's careful coordination of speech and action in this play. Examples abound in the abdication scene: Edward's despair is expressed in "Here, take my crowne, the life of *Edward* too," (l. 2043), and then his defiance in "See monsters see, ile weare my crowne againe" (l. 2060). The whole speech in which he does finally part with the crown is vividly

10. The most practical way of staging the murder, if the spit is to be used, is with Edward's head towards the audience. The table will then considerably obscure Lightborn's use of the spit, which he can silently take from the discovery-space and allow the spectators to see in his hands.

11. *Edward the Second* (*The New Mermaids*, London, 1967), p. 104.

dramatized, when he urges whoever most wishes his death to take it from his head, and of course nobody stirs. He goes on:

> What are you moovde, pitie you me?
> Then send for unrelenting *Mortimer*
> And *Isabell*, whose eyes being turnd to steele,
> Will sooner sparkle fire then shed a teare:
> Yet stay, for rather then I will looke on them,
> Heere, heere. (ll. 2088–93)

Having resigned the crown, he produces what must be a handkerchief:

> Beare this to the queene,
> Wet with my teares, and dried againe with sighes,
> If with the sight thereof she be not mooved,
> Returne it backe and dip it in my bloud. (ll. 2104–7)

Probably Marlowe was remembering the bloodstained handkerchief which Hieronimo carries as a memento of his revenge and accidentally offers another bereaved father to dry his tears with;[12] or, possibly, the one dipped in Rutland's blood which Queen Margaret savagely gives to the weeping captive York in *Henry VI Part 3*.[13] The next person to enter is Bartley: to the question "What newes bringes he?" Edward (who has just been anticipating that his murder will follow his abdication), rejoins

> Such newes as I expect: come *Bartley*, come,
> And tell thy message to my naked brest, (ll. 2116–17)

evidently opening his doublet as if to an assassin's dagger. What Bartley in fact brings is a letter removing Edward from Leicester's keeping. Edward asks Bartley,

> *Edw.* And who must keepe mee now, must you my lorde?
> *Bart.* I, my most gratious lord, so tis decreed.
> *Edw.* By *Mortimer*, whose name is written here.
> Well may I rent his name, that rends my hart,
> This poore revenge hath something easd my minde.
> (ll. 2124–8)

12. *The Spanish Tragedy*, III. xiii. 85.
13. *3 Henry VI*, I. iv. 79.

T. W. Craik

The business of the whole scene, though fully and naturally linked with the lines, is sufficiently reminiscent of *The Spanish Tragedy* to suggest that Marlowe had learned the technique from Kyd. Besides the use of the handkerchief, the actions involving the crown and the paper recall two incidents in Kyd's play. In the former, the Viceroy of Portugal throws himself to the ground in grief at Balthazar's presumed death, saying "Heere let me lye, now am I at the lowest" (I. iii. 14); but then he adds that he may sink still further:

> Yes, Fortune may bereave me of my Crowne:
> Heere take it now, (I. iii. 18–19)

evidently putting it off his head, for at the end of the scene, threatening Alexandro, he is directed to *Take the crown and put it on again*, with

> I, this was it that made thee spill his bloud,
> But Ile now weare it till thy bloud be spilt. (I. iii. 86–7)

In the second of the two scenes, that of Hieronimo and the petitioners, the hero is crazed with grief at his encounter with that other old man whose son has been murdered, and invites him to accompany him on a quest for justice from the underworld:

> Come on old Father be my *Orpheus*,
> And if thou canst no notes upon the Harpe,
> Then sound the burden of thy sore harts greefe,
> Till we do gaine that *Proserpine* may graunt
> Revenge on them that murd[e]red my Sonne,
> Then will I rent and tear them thus and thus,
> Shivering their limmes in peeces with my teeth.
> *Teare the Papers.* (III. xiii. 117–23)

I have quoted the lines, and developed the general resemblance to Kyd, in order to suggest that it is at least possible that Edward too tears Mortimer's letter with his teeth, although I would urge the greatest caution in using the argument of analogy when a piece of action is not so well established as to form a convention.

Such a convention is indicated by the direction, after Gaveston's banishment, *Enter king Edward moorning*, and his opening line, "Hees gone, and for his absence thus I moorne" (l. 602). The

86

traditional posture of grief, in poetry as well as drama, was to fold one's arms: Pandare appears thus when he tells Troilus of the decision to send Criseyde away,[14] and in Marlowe's time Astrophel and Stella show their sorrow "with arms crost";[15] we recall, too, John Ford the dramatist "with folded arms and melancholy hat"[16] and a number of Shakespearean references[17] come to mind. Obviously the convention was so familiar that Marlowe did not need to specify the posture.

I turn now to another incident in *Edward II* in which Marlowe has used dialogue and action together, this time to express the mutual relations of three characters: Edward, his favourite Gaveston, and his queen Isabel. Throughout the play he makes significant use of salutations, from the formal kneeling of a vassal to his lord to the embrace and kiss between lovers. This motif is present in the opening lines, when Gaveston has returned from exile at the new king's invitation: he could, he says in soliloquy, have swum from France,

> And like *Leander* gaspt upon the sande,
> So thou wouldst smile and take me in thy armes. (ll. 8–9)

He loves London only because it contains "The king, upon whose bosome let me die" (l. 14); he resolves not to stoop to the peers: "My knee shall bowe to none but to the king" (l. 19). As soon as the opportunity offers, he greets the king, who exclaims

> What *Gaveston*, welcome: kis not my hand,
> Embrace me *Gaveston* as I do thee:
> Why shouldst thou kneele, knowest thou not who I am? (ll. 140–2)

Shortly afterwards we hear from the Queen how Edward neglects her for Gaveston:

> He claps his cheekes, and hanges about his neck,
> Smiles in his face, and whispers in his eares,
> And when I come, he frownes, as who should say,
> Go whether thou wilt seeing I have Gaveston. (ll. 258–61)

---

14. Chaucer, *Troilus and Criseyde*, IV. 359.
15. Sidney, *Astrophel and Stella*, eighth song, line 19.
16. In the seventeenth-century *Times' Poets* (anonymous) quoted by Gifford and most of Ford's biographers. A portrait of John Donne in the National Portrait Gallery, London, shows him in such a pose (and such a hat).
17. *Tempest*, I. ii. 224; *Two G.*, II. i. 18; *L.L.L.*, III. i. 18, 171; IV. iii. 131–2.

T. W. Craik

That this is true is shown in action after Gaveston's new banishment. This is the incident I wish to analyse. Edward is taking leave of him and they exchange pictures; these are miniatures, which one hangs about one's neck, in one's bosom, so all the earlier business-and-dialogue is recalled when Edward says

> O might I keepe thee heere, as I doe this,
> Happie were I, but now most miserable. (ll. 424–5)

After a "dum imbracement," Edward insists on bringing Gaveston on his way. Their movement towards the exit is the cue for the Queen's entry:

Qu. Whether goes my lord?
Edw. Fawne not on me French strumpet, get thee gone. (ll. 440–1)

The whole dialogue shows the Queen's approaches repulsed. Its climax is:

Qu. Wherein my lord, have I deservd these words?
Witnesse the teares that *Isabella* sheds,
Witnesse this hart, that sighing for thee breakes,
How deare my lord is to poore *Isabell*.
Edw. And witnesse heaven how deere thou art to me.
There weepe, for till my *Gaveston* be repeald,
Assure thy selfe thou comst not in my sight.
Exeunt Edward and Gaveston. (ll. 459–65)

What is the stage business here? Glynne Wickham is in no doubt:

> The structure, pace and emotion of the scene demands [*sic*] that what Edward calls Heaven (and Isabella) to witness in line 167 [463 in the above quotation] is his physical relationship with Gaveston. What he should do at this point therefore is to walk slowly and deliberately to Gaveston and kiss him on the mouth, leaving the Queen to recoil in horror at the truth now wholly revealed.[18]

This surprises me, the more because Wickham has already insisted that the Queen's entry interrupts an embrace, not an exit as I believe; were that true, one would think the Queen had little left to learn, and in any case she can be in no doubt of the relationship,

18. *Shakespeare's Dramatic Heritage* (London, 1969), p. 174.

since her own earlier speech has made it quite clear. I should like to propose an altogether simpler reading. She succeeds in throwing her arms about Edward, and he throws or strikes her to the ground. "There weepe," he tells her – there on the floor where she is lying; and when the nobles come in, their lines tell the same story:

> *Lanc.* Looke where the sister of the king of Fraunce,
> Sits wringing of her hands, and beats her brest.
> *Warw.* The king I feare hath ill intreated her. (ll. 483–5)

However, in the most recent production I saw (by the Prospect Theatre in 1970), Wickham's suggestion had been acted upon, and I am afraid that the natural reading of the lines may now have a hard fight before it is accepted by producers.[19]

From tragic passions we turn to farce. Everyone remembers that the Horse-courser pulls off Faustus' leg when he is trying to wake him in order to complain that the horse he bought for forty dollars has changed into a bundle of hay. Faustus is asleep in a chair at the time. Greg points out that the chair is specified in the Quarto of 1604 (*Sleepe in his chaire*) even though a little earlier some lines peculiar to that text have mentioned "this faire and pleasant greene," and he remarks that "there is no reason why Faustus should not sit down and fall asleep by the way-side."[20] If the incident is considered as narrative there is indeed no reason, but if it is considered as action there may be a very good reason, because I conjecture that in the chair Faustus will find a rug to throw over his legs, and wrapped in this rug will be the extra leg which, during his six-line soliloquy, he will manipulate so that the foot protrudes ready for the Horse-courser's grasp. Looked at in this way, the speech "What art thou Faustus but a man condemnd to die?" becomes a means to an end, rather than an end in itself.[21]

19. In this production (by Toby Robertson) Edward had prematurely thrown Isabella to the floor at "Away then, touch me not" (l. 455). At "And witnesse heaven how deere thou art to me," he made as if to kiss her, reached out his hand meanwhile to Gaveston and then kissed him instead.
20. *Marlowe's Doctor Faustus, 1604–1616.* Parallel texts edited by W. W. Greg (Oxford, 1950), p. 59.
21. Alternatively, Faustus could conceal the false leg under his long gown (which he raises to show the clowns he has recovered his leg: Q1616, Appendix to *Dr. Faustus*, ll. 1361–2). Even in Q1616 this would involve walking on with it and playing twenty-five lines, while in Q1604 he would have to play the whole scene at the Emperor's court, since he does not leave the stage between that scene and the Horse-courser's entry.

T. W. Craik

For my final illustration I turn to the scene in which the Old Man, who has tried in vain to get Faustus to repent, is threatened by devils. This is at Faustus' command: Mephostophilis, accepting the order, has replied

> His faith is great, I cannot touch his soule,
> But what I may afflict his body with,
> I wil attempt, which is but little worth. (ll. 1316–8)

There intervenes Faustus' address to Helen, at the end of which the Old Man reappears and sadly apostrophizes the departing sinner. Then

> *Enter the Divelles.*
> Sathan begins to sift me with his pride:
> As in this furnace God shal try my faith,
> My faith, vile hel, shal triumph over thee.
> Ambitious fiends, see how the heavens smiles
> At your repulse, and laughs your state to scorne.
> Hence hel, for hence I flie unto my God. *Exeunt.* (ll. 1351–6)

In the source, the Old Man is physically unharmed by anything that Mephostophilis can do to him, and I am sure that Greg is right when he takes this to be the dramatist's intention in these lines, though he points out that there is a possible uncertainty as to "whether what is represented is the Old Man's triumph or his martyrdom."[22] From the lines themselves it may not be certain, but the combined evidence of the source, of the rest of the play, and of the implied stage business at this point, makes it clear that the Old Man does not die. If he were killed, the devils would have razed his skin to some purpose, and the Good Angel's earlier assurance to Faustus that *his* skin would be safe if he repented would be retrospectively undermined. Moreover, if the Old Man were killed, his spiritual triumph would rest on his words alone: his soul could not be shown to fly unto his God, and, as for his body, what would become of that? The unthinkable alternative, the devils carrying it off, would make him look not only thoroughly dead but thoroughly damned. Having determined that the Old Man triumphs in the flesh as well as in the spirit, we have still to determine how his triumph is achieved. It looks from his last line

22. *Marlowe's Doctor Faustus, 1604–1616*, pp. 389–90.

as though he and the devils go out at opposite doors after their "repulse." As Greg remarks, he has "a rather easy victory." I suppose he must make some gesture, from which the devils dramatically recoil because it exhibits his faith. The obvious traditional gesture would be to cross himself, were it not that this was hilariously ineffectual when the Pope did it at his banquet in an earlier scene. Nevertheless, this may just possibly be what he does, for the play is not so self-consistent, nor so uncompromisingly anti-Catholic, as to forbid it. An alternative gesture, more acceptable to Protestants but less theatrically impressive, would be to join his hands in prayer.

To attempt to sum up the principles involved in the reconstruction of each of these pieces of stage action would take almost as long as their analysis, so I hope you will permit me to summarize in general terms. I have not tried to claim that there is a single correct way of establishing the stage action: simply to remind you that there are various kinds of evidence that can be interpreted, and that the interpreter's task is to maintain his imagination and his discretion in proper balance. To do this sort of thing at all, one must be excited by the plays and wish to visualize them in action. Another reason why the subject is of absorbing interest is that one can debate with oneself. And a further one is that, although we can hardly hope to find conclusive proof, we can reasonably hope to find corroboration; the ideal interpreter of problems of action, therefore, like the ideal interpreter of problems of text, will read each play with every other Elizabethan play simultaneously in mind. This is, admittedly, the ideal and not the reality, but it is an ideal worth pursuing.

The Oddity of Lyly's
Endimion

PETER SACCIO

When I last wrote on the court comedies of John Lyly, I trod with some delicacy around his most famous play. Unwilling to found my theories of Lyly's art upon so controverted a piece, and anxious in any case to point out the virtues of other plays, I discussed *Endimion* in a series of tentative suggestions carefully placed after the development of my major argument. I am delighted to have the present opportunity to reconsider the play and in particular to face as directly as I can whatever it is that makes *Endimion* a puzzling experience.

I have argued that Lyly's mythological comedies may be divided, on the basis of their dramaturgy, into two groups.[1] Three of them, *Sapho and Phao* (1584), *Gallathea* (1585), and *Love's Metamorphosis* (c. 1589), are notably lacking in action. Their scenes explore analogous situations arranged in a pattern that might be compared to the polyptic structure of a Renaissance altarpiece. In *Gallathea*, for example, there are three such situations, each hinging upon the defiance of a god. Shepherds attempt to cheat Neptune of an appointed virgin-sacrifice by disguising their eligible daughters; Cupid causes the nymphs of Diana to fall

1. The succeeding generalizations on Lyly's dramaturgy are summarized from my *Court Comedies of John Lyly: A Study in Allegorical Dramaturgy* (Princeton, 1969). All quotations from Lyly are drawn from *The Complete Works of John Lyly*, ed. R. Warwick Bond (Oxford, 1902; reprinted 1967), with i/j and u/v altered to conform to modern usage. I wish to thank, for their criticism and suggestions, not only those attending the Elizabethan Theatre Conference, but also Professors James Cox and Peter Travis of Dartmouth College and Robert Grams Hunter of Vanderbilt University.

in love and thus to defy the rule of their goddess; and the nymphs, once Diana has cured their infatuations, capture Cupid and set him to tasks that violate his nature as god of love. Such development as occurs within this largely static structure depends upon the wealth of potential meaning within the gods. The nature and relationships of love, chastity and destiny, the forces imaged by the gods of *Gallathea*, are slowly developed, defined and enriched during the progress of the play. The gradual exfoliation of these divine figures prompted me to term the mode of meaning employed in the play "allegory of the expanding image." By contrast, Lyly's last two mythological comedies, *Midas* (1590) and *The Woman in the Moon* (c. 1593), manifest an increasing emphasis on narrative. The polyptic structure is largely, though not completely, abandoned in favour of sequential action presented with a greater interest in causal linkage, accelerating intrigue, the consequences of decisions, and similar plot values. In *Midas*, for example, Lyly produces a serial dramatization of the two Ovidian tales, the golden touch and the ass's ears. In these plays allegorical implications do not develop throughout; they are usually suggested, by way of dramatic preparation, somewhere mid-play, but their full impact is reserved for the denouement, a moment of radical vision that alters the entire context of the preceding action. At the end of *Midas*, in a theophany of universal harmony, Apollo blazes forth at his own temple in Delphi. The fact that these plays, and certain contemporary court comedies by other playwrights, end in such significant theophanies, prompted me to label their mode of meaning "allegory of the anagogic denouement."

Although these groupings of Lyly's mythological comedies still appear to me valid, the position of *Endimion* (c. 1588) within them is uncertain. Classification with the first set is invited by the static nature of the play. The story is slight: in a reversal of the Greek myth, Endimion loves an unaware Cynthia. He soliloquizes for two acts and then falls asleep; his sleep is prolonged for another two acts by the craft of Dipsas, the witch hired by his jealous former love, Tellus. His friend Eumenides, seeking a cure, is told by a magical fountain that the kiss of Cynthia will waken him; condescending, she bestows the kiss, grants him her favour, and pairs the rest of the cast off in a series of marriages. As this story is worked into scenes, the principal male lovers, Endimion, Eumenides and Sir Tophas (the protagonist of the parodic subplot), are all held apart from their respective ladies until the last scene; thus, although they strike attitudes and speak at great length, their feelings precipitate little action. A large cast, mathematically elaborated in pairs and oppositions, turns before us like a display case in a gold museum, each glittering object neatly separated from the next. The real development of the play lies in our increasing understanding of Cynthia. She is identified at first merely as the Moon; gradually we discover her also to be a human queen; only in the final scene is her sovereignty fully exercised. The image expands in the manner of Lyly's earlier gods.

On the other hand, various elements of *Endimion* invite classification with Lyly's later mythological comedies, the comedies of stronger narrative line climaxed by anagogical display. In the first two acts of the play there is an attempt, slight but unusual for Lyly, at linking scenes. Three scenes (I.ii, I.iii, II.ii) begin with direct comment upon the situation concluding the previous scene, almost as if the entering characters had overheard their predecessors on stage. Further, as G. K. Hunter has observed,[2] the action as a whole contains a series of motifs that bring *Endimion* closer than Lyly's other plays to medieval romance: the dramatically "strong" elements of a witch threatening to unleash chaos, the enchanted sleeper guarded by fairies, the estranged lover Geron who has lived as a hermit for fifty years, and the magical fountain that grants a true lover a single wish. Finally, although Cynthia is continuously a subject of discussion through the play, her appearances on the stage are handled in a pattern characteristic of the later court plays. Whereas the gods of *Gallathea* appear throughout the action, Lyly gives Cynthia only one short scene in Act III before her closing displays of power. Thus he anticipates the method of *Midas* and the anonymous *Maid's Metamorphosis*, where the appearances of the presiding god are strictly rationed to a mid-play introduction and a final theophany. This careful restriction of Cynthia's on-stage role greatly influences her effect upon us. We see little of the quotidian in her; expressions of awe and reverence from other characters lead us to a figure who is wholly queen and goddess. To sum up, *Endimion* appears to belong to both my categories.

Now dispute over the grouping of Lyly's plays may resemble a

2. G. K. Hunter, *John Lyly: The Humanist as Courtier* (Cambridge, Mass., 1962), p. 192.

squabble over the proper shape of keystones by those attempting to build a Gothic arch out of junket. Compared with the plays of Marlowe, Shakespeare or Jonson, those of Lyly initially strike the reader as so homogeneous that their variety, both within a given play and across the canon, may easily escape notice. Nevertheless, the differences are there, and various schemes of classification have been proposed: the Victorian division into "historical," "pastoral," "allegorical" and "realistic"; Hunter's categories of "unification round debate" and "harmonious variety"; my two sorts of allegory. In the present context, one fact about these proposals is notable: *Endimion* has regularly been an obstacle to clear ordering. The play provoked Victorian and early twentieth-century critics into notorious excesses of topical and doctrinal allegory, provoked some of them so sharply that they endeavoured to drag *Midas*, *Sapho and Phao* and *The Woman in the Moon* up the same garden path. Hunter, seeking Lyly's methods of unification, considered *Endimion* a debate play, and then honestly conceded that debate had here shrunk to a minor motif. I, trying to parcel the canon according to structure and mode of meaning, must confess that *Endimion* bridges my two major kinds. Despite the fact that *Endimion* has been more frequently reprinted and anthologized than Lyly's other plays and has, I take it, been therefore offered in many courses as a characteristic example of Elizabethan court drama, it proves to be an oddity even in that secluded world.

II

The oddity of *Endimion*, suggested by its defeat of the critical systems that have tried to contain it, can be traced to fundamental elements of play-writing. In this play Lyly modifies or departs from his usual practices in setting, in characterization, and in the kinds of action chosen for presentation.

Endimion occurs in a remarkably undefined setting. Normally, Lyly's plays occur in a specific location: *Campaspe* in Athens, for example, or *Midas* in Phrygia with the final scene at Delphi. These places are of course imaginatively rather than archeologically constructed, with varying quantities of particular detail, but they are nonetheless definite geographical settings. *Gallathea* and *Love's Metamorphosis* occur in the conventional world of pastoral, this world in the case of *Gallathea* being amusingly located on the banks of the River Humber. But where does Cynthia rule? Over all the earth, as long as she is called the Moon. Over a specific country, one assumes, when she sends her courtiers to Egypt, Greece and Thessaly, but that country is as placeless as Spenser's Faerie Land, and nameless to boot. *Endimion* affords us an extreme example of the Elizabethan lack of concern with the fictional location of dramatic action. We merely observe a stage where people meet and talk. We are in what Coleridge called "mental space."[3]

Now the lack of a definite fictional location may be of minor significance; this is a play and we do have a stage. At the court performance that stage was presumably decorated in accordance with the usual practice of the Revels Office, with several "houses" arranged in the pattern known as multiple staging. Lyly usually arranges a triangle of "houses" (some of them actually not habitations) around which the blocking can be organized: in *Campaspe* the palace of Alexander, the shop of Apelles, and the tub of Diogenes; in *Love's Metamorphosis* the temple of Cupid, the rock of a seductive Siren, and the arborified nymph of chastity. These sets develop symbolic significance through the play, coming to embody ideas or ways of life associated with the various characters.[4] The text of *Endimion* seems to call for two, perhaps three, such houses. Geron explicitly denies having any lodging in his place of hermitage, but he is of course discovered beside his magical fountain, the focus for one long and important scene. The focus for three, perhaps four, scenes is the lunary bank upon which Endimion sleeps.[5] The dialogue concerning the bank, however, presents several puzzles about its appearance. Corsites undertakes to remove the sleeping Endimion from what he calls a "Caban" (IV.iii.111), presumably some temporary hut constructed at Cynthia's orders to shelter her courtier. But how is this cabin arranged with respect to the tree upon which Endimion apparently reposes? Eumenides, endeavouring to convince the awakened Endimion of the reality of his experience, remarks, "Behold, the twig to which thou laidst thy head, is now become a tree" (V. i. 51–52). (One would like to know just how this transformation was man-

3. S. T. Coleridge, *Miscellaneous Criticism*, ed. T. M. Raysor (London, 1936), p. 36.
4. Fuller discussion of Lyly's staging, with references, may be found in *Court Comedies*, Chapter I.
5. II.iii, IV.iii, and V.i use the lunary bank. It is difficult to tell how close the actors should come to the bank in IV.ii.

aged! And is this the same tree that is de-arborified into Bagoa in the closing lines of the play?) There may be a third house, less important in the action than the others: two scenes between Corsites and Tellus occur at the castle to which she is exiled, the first beginning with the only explicit reference: "Heere is the Castle . . . in which you must weave" (III.ii.1). On the public stage such a line would merely accompany a gesture at the tiring-house facade; on the court stage of the 1580s it probably indicates a genuine set-piece.

Two things are missing from this conjectured set. Lyly's other sets include houses for the dominant character of each play, an obvious stage realization of that character's sovereignty: Alexander's palace, Neptune's sacred oak in *Gallathea*, Cupid's temple in *Love's Metamorphosis*, and so forth. No word in *Endimion* hints at a palace for Cynthia, Lyly's most regal figure. I can suppose an upstage palace through whose facade she enters and leaves; I can imagine it spectacular, laden with symbolic motifs; it might even do double-duty as Tellus' castle of exile; but there is no evidence that it existed. Now in part I am merely complaining about a scholarly difficulty. That we do not know enough to reconstruct satisfactorily what the court audience saw is regrettable, but Lyly did not write his dialogue to tell us what his stage looked like, and our ignorance does not alter the fact that the first audience saw something that contributed to their experience of the play. But in part I am remarking upon an inherent quality of *Endimion*. The second thing that strikes me as missing is something larger than a single piece of decor, namely Lyly's characteristic particularity. His is a world of concrete objects, of sharp empirical realities. He strives ever after pattern, but his patterns are built upon the hard factual existence of things. He makes "hustling details calmed and relevant,"[6] and this specificity is as notable in his stage settings as in the Elizabethan menagerie of his similes. The lack of textual reference to stage setting not only creates scholarly uncertainty now; it also reduced the potential significance of whatever set-pieces appeared on the original stage. A putative Cynthian palace, however spectacular or symbolic, could have had great initial impact but would not have developed in the meaning of the play. Sets to which attention is not called at key

6. Thom Gunn, "A Mirror for Poets," *Fighting Terms* (London, 1962).

moments tend to fade away into mere background. Cupid's temple, Neptune's oak, Apelles' paintings – for that matter, Shylock's scales and Falstaff's cushion – gain meaning for an audience because they are brought into the action and dialogue. Thus Geron's fountain for one scene, Endimion's lunary bank for three or four, and perhaps Tellus' castle for two, have importance. The remaining ten or eleven scenes occur nowhere in particular, and these include all of the first six scenes of the play, a stretch of unlocated action unmatched elsewhere in the surviving court drama. The curious placelessness of *Endimion* is a matter of stage presentation as well as of fictional locale. *Endimion* is like a dream in which for a time a single vivid object gives us our only sense of place, and often we are in no particular place at all.

A more subtle aspect of the play's dreamlike quality lies in the nature of certain characters. Again a comparison with Lyly's other comedies is instructive. *Campaspe* presents extensive social particularity: king, lieutenant, artist, philosopher, noblewoman, pageboy and lowborn virgin dance a precise pavane of decorous relationship. Lyly's succeeding plays, although displaying less social range and less social concern, still shelve their characters in neat and recognizable niches: scholar, courtier, shepherd, god. With several major characters in *Endimion*, however, we are left to wonder where in the hierarchy of the universe they belong. To misquote Shakespeare's song, "Who is Cynthia? What is she?"

In the first scene, Endimion describes himself as literally in love with the Moon. Not a word touching Cynthia hints that she is anything other than the astronomical body, the Moon itself. Eumenides naturally considers him mad. We are not, or not yet, in the realm of a human queen, else the rationalist Eumenides would understand what lies beneath his friend's extravagant metaphor. It is therefore not, or not yet, metaphor. Cynthia is not spoken of as a "Ladie," a human being capable (in Dipsas' opinion) of mistrust and jealousy, until the closing lines of Act I (I.iv.37–41). Endimion continues his extravagant adoration in Act II. The Moon imagery persists, but it is oddly mingled with language suggesting that Cynthia is a being whose favour can be won: he promises romantic exploits that will achieve her kindness. It seems vain to fish for definitions in the river of Endimion's rapture. Endimion then meets with Tellus, who resentfully attempts to strip Cynthia of remarkable attributes. Their wit-combat leads to a passage of breath-taking stichomythia, a passage demonstrating Lyly's extra-ordinary ability to combine mythological playfulness with stark sublimity:

> *Tellus.* Why, she is but a woman.
> *End.* No more was *Venus.*
> *Tellus.* Shee is but a virgin.
> *End.* No more was *Vesta.*
> *Tellus.* Shee shall have an ende.
> *End.* So shall the world.
> *Tellus.* Is not her beautie subject to time?
> *End.* No more then time is to standing still.
> *Tellus.* Wilt thou make her immortall?
> *End.* No, but incomparable. (II.i.79–88)

She is not strictly a goddess, then, but not a mere mortal either. She is incomparable; we cannot assign her a status in the universe that another being might share. Her status cannot be defined; indeed, Endimion declares that no one can "comprehend" her salient characteristic, "Majestie" (II.iii.16–18). She can be described only by poetic imagery, and the clearest, most elaborately maintained image for her is the first: she is the Moon. Dwelling in the sphere that divides the eternal from the transitory, she combines within herself the eternal and the transitory. She focuses the influence of the lasting gods upon the sea that ebbs and flows and the earth that fructifies and decays. It is her miracle to change and yet be *semper eadem.*[7]

When Cynthia finally appears in Act III, a radical shift occurs in her presentation, the most important aspect of which is theatrical. Instead of merely hearing her praises, we see her, played by a choirboy of Paul's. Aside from special magnificence of costume, she must have looked like anyone else. A queen, no doubt, addressed as "Madame," but human, and no less tart in rebuking the quarrelsomeness of her ladies than they are in quarrelling. But the passage is short, only sixty lines, and Cynthia retreats to reassume the position of adored, remote, unseen power, the miracle-worker to whom the fountain directs Eumenides. She does not reappear until the final scenes: there she is all grace and condescension in the revival of Endimion, all justice and mercy in the closing trial.

7. I am here summarizing Endimion's principal descriptions of Cynthia in I.i and II.ii.

The Moon imagery vanishes, to be replaced by overtones of Christian divinity. The key words, emphasized by great repetition, are no longer astronomical but theological, drawn from the allegory of the Daughters of God: Cynthia establishes "truth," threatens wrongdoers with "justice," and finally grants "mercie" to all. Instead of focusing upon earth the influences of astronomical powers, she represents on earth the functions of Christian deity. The Moon becomes God's anointed, restoring love among men and women, and between mankind and herself.[8]

This shimmering ineffability in Cynthia, this cursive variation in the handling of the central character, does not occur elsewhere in Lyly. Elsewhere mortals are mortals and gods gods. In part the odd treatment undoubtedly results from Lyly's desire to compliment the queen who was the play's primary audience, to compliment her even more extravagantly than he did in creating the strictly human Sapho. Royal compliment, however, cannot entirely account for the unusual treatment of character, for the careful variation in her impact. The desire to compliment does not of itself determine the form compliment is to take. Lyly does not in any case thrust flattery into his plays like plums in a pudding; the plays have their independent inner rationale, compliment arising unobtrusively from the whole. Furthermore, the peculiarity of Cynthia's status affects other persons in the play: daemonic qualities exist also in Dipsas and Tellus. They are not sustained;

8. That the Daughters of God are present in *Endimion* has been suggested by Bernard Huppé ("Allegory of Love in Lyly's Court Comedies," *ELH*, XIV [1947], 105n.) and J. A. Bryant, Jr. ("The Nature of the Allegory in Lyly's *Endymion*," *Renaissance Papers*, Southeastern Renaissance Conference [1956], pp. 7–8). I have pursued these suggestions, attempting to identify the three ladies of Endimion's dream with particular Daughters and with various female characters in the play (*Court Comedies*, pp. 175–185). Huppé has replied, sketching another possibility within the sharp space restriction of a review, and justifiably cautious because of the discrepancy in number between the three dream-ladies and the traditionally four Daughters (*RQ*, XXIII [1970], 479). I now think that my earlier interpretation was unwarrantably elaborate. That the three dream-ladies behave like the Daughters of God, and thus prepare us for later possible meanings, is unquestionable. Our ignorance of how they were costumed, and Lyly's own refusal to interpret them (V.i.94–95) make it difficult to say anything more about them. The *significance* of the Daughters of God is called upon only in the final scene, where the words "justice," "mercy," and "truth" are emphasized in connection with Cynthia's sovereignty. Far more important than details of number and diagrammatic identification is the question of timing, of when Lyly chooses to draw in these potential significances.

after Act II these women are women merely, abject and defence-less before Cynthia. In the opening scenes, however, they possess larger dimensions that make them temporarily able to oppose Cynthia.

Dipsas requires only brief remark. She claims omnipotence with but one limitation: she cannot rule hearts (I.iv.24). Significantly, the boast of the source character, Ovid's Dipsas, has been heightened. Ovid's bawd can alter the weather and turn the stars blood-red;[9] Lyly's witch can "darken the Sunne . . . remoove the Moone out of her course . . . restore youth to the aged, and make hils without bottoms" (I.iv.20–22). Her power is of course demonstrated on stage in Endimion's sleep and Bagoa's transformation.

Tellus is more complex. It is usually pointed out that her name means "Earth," that she is therefore opposed to Cynthia the Moon, and that this opposition may be translated into a pair of rival bids for Endimion's allegiance, some variation on the notion of the two Venuses. I find this over-schematic, as if one were to mistake for London itself the conventional diagram of the Underground. The contrast with Cynthia is glancing and indirect, not an opposition of equals. Tellus appears on stage, describing herself as "a woman" (I.ii.52), long before Cynthia ceases being an entirely off-stage Moon. Concerning her name there is an odd point of technique. If, instead of taking a bird's-eye view of the play, we attend to the sequence of impressions as they are given us, we will notice that Lyly does not mention her name in the spoken dialogue until the end of Act I (I.iv.29). He here departs from his regular practice of distributing vocatives copiously through the speeches; for once he allows his audience, as Spenser frequently does, to see the character in action, speech and description before supplying the name. As a result, the name Tellus does not serve as a banderole, a definitive label whose capital letters may block deeper acquaintance with the character, but as a handle by which we may more easily carry a wealth of experience. By the time we arrive at the name, we have seen much in Tellus, some of it making little sense in connection with the literal Earth. True, she has a remarkable speech claiming that her "body is decked with faire flowers" and that her "vaines are Vines, yeelding sweet liquor to the dullest spirits" (I.ii.20–21). True, she is beautiful, as the Earth is beautiful.

9. *Amores*, I.8. Lyly's source in Ovid was pointed out by R. G. Howarth, "Dipsas in Lyly and Marston," *N&Q*, CLXXV (1938), 24–25.

But when she threatens to entangle Endimion in nets of pleasure, amorous devices, and loose desires (I.ii.40–50), we move away from Earth to earthiness. Her jealousy moves us further, for jealousy is a spiritual perversion. Finally she comes to a resolution: if she cannot have Endimion, "it shall suffice me if the world talke that I am favoured" of him (I.ii.73). Placing such a value upon fame, gossip, is a quality we call, not earthiness, but worldliness. The name is rich. We would perhaps do more justice to the resonance of the name and the role were we to review the extensive list of epithets that Cooper culls out of the classics for his *Thesaurus* entry under *tellus*, or were we to remember the passage in 1 Corinthians 15 where St. Paul, in a few verses, goes all the way from asserting "the glory of the terrestrial" to describing Adam as "of the earth, earthy," that is, born of the dust and fallen. Thus Tellus, although not as near divinity as Cynthia, is yet a little larger than ordinary human beings. The size is complemented by energy: she plots continuously and single-mindedly. The sharp edge of her character is malice, a quality so frequently pointed out in her that it becomes her hallmark, as majesty is Cynthia's.[10] In her size, her evil energy, her ceaseless schemes for harm (not all of them acted upon), Tellus has a good deal of the Vice-figure about her. She is the only non-comic character in Lyly of whom that might be said.

I have endeavoured to point out a dreamlike quality in the setting of *Endimion*, and a daemonic quality in its major female characters. To complete my discussion of the oddity of the play, I shall turn to one more component of its dramaturgy. In the varying modes of its action *Endimion* is especially odd. To refer once more to Lyly's other plays, the court comedies are usually constructed in many short scenes that inspect a complex world built upon an elaborate architecture of idea rather than a strong story line. Since the action of each play is but a gallery of anecdotes, and since the coolly glamorous characters, far from inviting our emotional participation, present their cases in a series of elegant debates and polished poses, our attention is drawn to the interrelationship of notions and the coherent grace of manners. A corollary of this euphuistic playwriting is the absence of intense moral pressure.

10. That the words "malice" and "malicious" are used of Tellus nine times was pointed out by Edward S. Le Comte, *Endymion in England* (New York, 1944), p. 75n.

We do not assist in dilemmas of reason and passion; we do not witness characters approaching difficult choices or suffering the results of their decisions. Choice, the turning point of moral experience, becomes intellectual dilemma, and potential emotional crisis becomes design. Again, *Endimion* fails to fit easily into generalizations evolved to describe the other plays. As I remarked earlier, although *Endimion* shares with the earlier comedies their mathematical elaboration, their polyptic survey of a various world, it has suffered an infusion of motifs from romantic narrative, gaining occasions of stronger plot and more powerful dramatic impact. This unevenness in what might be called the texture of the action, this occasional acceleration from static configuration into romantic episode, is particularly noticeable in two scenes, the early encounter of Endimion and Tellus, and Eumenides' choice at the fountain.

The scene between Tellus and Endimion at the beginning of Act II could have been a standard Lylian encounter, exploring but not advancing a complex situation. In part, it is written that way. It begins with one of Endimion's long soliloquies; when Tellus enters each character announces in an aside the intention to dissemble; there ensues some wit-combat upon the relation between deceit and female sex; this leads to the stichomythia upon Cynthia quoted above; and Endimion closes the scene by claiming that his love for Cynthia is merely the humble adoration appropriate to their respective ranks. By the formula, we ought to have gotten nowhere. But, oddly, an event has taken place, an event with murky implications. Endimion has lied. In the soliloquy, Endimion has confessed that, during his seven years of devotion to Cynthia, he has dissembled with Tellus, "using her but as a cloake for mine affections" (II.i.23). His subsequent declaration to Tellus, that "the sweet remembrance of your love, is the onely companion of my life" (II.i.53–54), is therefore flat falsehood. Tellus suspects the falsity sufficiently to force a revelation of his feeling for Cynthia. Now that is a fairly strong dramatic situation, strong enough to invite some moral question about Endimion. Why does he lie – a graceless deed in a Renaissance courtier? Does he really need a cloak for his affections? An uncomfortable, interesting, fertile event is taking place. In that context, the end of the scene looks very abrupt, as if Endimion were running away from Tellus. The relationship between the two characters is never wholly resolved.

Even the long trial scene at the end of the play does not clearly
establish the extent of Endimion's vows to Tellus, or whether they
had ever been sincere. (Some lines imply that Endimion's loves
were sequential – first Tellus, then Cynthia – so that the vows,
although eventually broken, were not perjured at the start.) It may
be that Lyly is simply careless here about story detail, as the
Elizabethans often were. But the effect of the carelessness, if it is
that, is notably strange. Lyly could have handled Tellus' jealousy
with no risk to Endimion's moral character simply by making her
love totally unrequited. Endimion would then have been poised
between Tellus and Cynthia with no sense of damaging compromise – a characteristic Lylian pattern. Instead, Lyly has begun
to invent a history for these relationships, and written a scene in
which one event of that history takes place. The history, the event,
have dramatic impact. When Tellus meets Endimion, Lyly is
hesitating between a simple *configuration*, a piece of significant
design involving static characters, and an *event*, an episode in a
developing romantic narrative featuring characters of a fuller
humanity.

But the strongest infusion of human reality and romantic event
lies in the role of Eumenides, particularly the scene at the fountain.
Lyly has placed at the exact centre of his usual anecdotal, polyptic
structure an exploit out of romance. Eumenides is a wandering
knight. He meets a hermit who is apparently doomed to remain by
his magical fountain until some one makes the fountain work. It
requires a faithful lover to tap the power of the fountain, and this
Eumenides is, but only after he has passed that first obstacle does
the real trial begin, the fountain's command, "*Aske one for all, and
but one thing at all*" (III.iv.81). That trial produces the characteristic Lylian debate: shall Eumenides choose love or friendship,
Semele or Endimion? But the debate differs from other Lylian
debates in two significant ways. First, it is an internal debate,
argued by a man who feels and tries to assess fairly both sides.
Geron contributes powerful advice, but the two characters are not
posed on opposite sides of the question in the usual Lylian manner.
Second, it is not an open-ended debate, issueless, set up merely to
explore juxtaposed values. The debate leads to decision and action.
It is a test. Here we reach the essential romantic character of the
scene; far more important than the hermit/fountain trappings is
the ordeal that is its action. Eumenides is questing at the command

of his queen; his success in overcoming the obstacles of that quest depend upon his own character; and the obstacles are provided by that standard romantic adversary, fortune.[11] At a moment when, unexpectedly, he could gain the woman he loves, everything depends upon his fidelity to the quest. In an exquisite doubling of the issue, he remains constant to the quest by preferring the constancy of friendship over the instability and mere fortune of love:

All thinges (friendship excepted) are subject to fortune: Love is but an eye-worme, which onely tickleth the heade with hopes and wishes: friendshippe the image of eternitie, in which there is nothing moveable, nothing mischeevous. (III.iv.122–6)

The fountain replies, of course, by invoking the power of constancy in its greatest and most paradoxical embodiment, Cynthia herself:

When shee whose figure of all is the perfectest, and never to bee measured – alwaies one, yet never the same – still inconstant, yet never wavering – shall come and kisse Endimion in his sleepe, he shall then rise; els never. (III.iv.155–8)

III

These things, then, make *Endimion* unique and difficult in the canon of Lyly's plays: odd formal characteristics, odd staging, odd handling of character and an odd blend of modes in its action. These oddities are, I think, functions of the play's subject, devices for showing forth the "*Idea* or foreconceite of the work."

The subject of *Endimion* is constancy, and it is realized in two ways. First, Lyly endeavours to present an embodiment of the virtue itself in the paradoxical figure of Cynthia. She is the quality conceived of as a universal. Thus she is divine, but she is also human because the divine constancy enters and affects the world. At the beginning the imagery is astronomical: the Moon controls the tides and fertilizes the earth. Through her the eternal forms enter the mutable world, and hence, although she waxes and wanes, she is ever the same. As human queen in Act III, she governs a court where people suffer and act under the influence

11. As a rule, Lyly does not make significant use of the notion of fortune in his plays, but in this scene the word "fortune" and its variants occur nine times, usually stressed.

of mutable passions. Hence the stress on Tellus' energy and Semele's tartness. Were such passions fully released they would destroy the credit of virtue and disrupt the workings of the world. In her final appearance Cynthia manifests the virtues of God's Daughters. The embodiment of constancy is referred to a context above the metaphysical forms that direct earthly process, to the ultimate divine constancy that governs the world in united justice, mercy and truth. To this extent the play is an act of exploration and an act of adoration in Lyly's usual polyptic style.

But constancy is a human virtue too, achievable by ordinary mortals. As such, its full presentation requires more than the stasis of early Lyly: it invites motifs of suffering and test. So the second part of Lyly's realization calls for something of a story, and it proves to be a story with two heroes. As human constancy can be a matter of unwavering, devoted attention, or a matter of unwavering, undiscouraged pursuit, as it can be contemplative or active, so Lyly invents his Endimion and his Eumenides, a beadsman and a knight. That is why the lunary bank and the fountain are the most important elements of the set: they give local habitation to the constancy of our two heroes. As beadsman, Endimion must simply remain single-minded. That is why Tellus' encounter with him is handled so much like an episode in a romance: it must be a strong onslaught. He persists in his devotion, a "solitarie life, almost these seaven yeeres" (II.i.14) until he is physically exhausted. "No rest *Endimion?*" he asks himself wearily at the beginning of his last soliloquy (II.iii.1). Dipsas' magic extends a sleep originally natural.[12] In the achievement of this solitary virtue,

12. I strenuously disagree with the nearly universal view that Endimion's sleep betokens Cynthia's disfavour. I therefore welcome David Bevington's conclusive demonstration that this common view is contradicted by the text; Cynthia is at first unaware of Endimion's bondage, and initiates the efforts to release him as soon as she is told. She neither criticizes him nor resents Tellus' love for him (*Tudor Drama and Politics* [Cambridge, Mass., 1968], pp. 179–180). Sir Henry Lee's entertainment at Woodstock of 1592, sometimes cited as analogous, in fact offers a useful contrast. In that piece, the Knight's sleep, a punishment for faithlessness, is imposed by the Fairy Queen herself. A better analogy for the genesis of Endimion's sleep lies in Sir Guyon's faint after three sleepless days of resisted temptation in the Cave of Mammon. Both Endimion and Guyon have pushed human capacity to the limit.

The disfavour interpretation has resulted, in part at least, from the habit of thinking of *Endimion* in terms of topical allegory. Although puzzling local passages in Lyly's plays may enshroud a few glancing topical allusions, Bevington and Hunter have argued against overall topical interpretations of

the great enemy is time. Lyly lays stress on the pathos of time; Endimion ages without ever having enjoyed the things of this world. (This is, of course, a departure from the myth: the Greek Endymion slept in eternal youth.) "Time . . . treadeth all things downe," remarks Dipsas, "all things . . . but trueth" (I.iv.47). But Endimion achieves his virtue. When Cynthia learns of his constancy, his truth, and grants him her favour, his age falls away. When achieved virtue is rewarded, we shall all be changed.

Eumenides is deliberately paired with Endimion. At the cost of inconsistency in the time-scheme of the play, he too has spent seven years silently adoring his mistress (III.iv.54). A mere Horatio in the first act, he steps forth after his friend has fallen asleep to become the knight of active constancy, while Sir Tophas and Corsites in different ways parody the role. This structural pattern bears some resemblance to the odd handling of the hero in Shakespeare's *Cymbeline*. Like Endimion, Posthumus disappears from the play between Acts II and V, leaving Imogen to bear the ordeal created by Iachimo's machinations, and leaving Cloten, dressed in his clothes, to parody his temporary jealousy.[13] Eumenides achieves the virtue doubly, constancy to his queen's command and constancy to Endimion's friendship – friendship, the "image of eternitie." For him, the enemy is not time but the things that time brings, fortune. He resists the unexpected opportunity to gain Semele at the expense of Endimion. Indeed, he even undergoes a final test of fidelity at the end of the play, offering to be mutilated in Semele's place when she is threatened with the queen's displeasure.

From a strategic point of view, then, we can see the peculiar dramaturgy is decreed by the demands of Lyly's subject. Constancy in its universal aspect can be presented by the usual static unfolding of scenes; constancy as a human virtue calls for events that tumble over in romantic narrative. *Endimion* is thus a halfway house, a Lylian hybrid, possessing both the slow revelation of universals that we witness in *Gallathea* and the education through

---

the plays so effectively that one can reasonably hope to hear no more of them. Bevington has written so well of the generalized devotion of these plays that I shall add nothing here on the way in which Cynthia is a celebration of Queen Elizabeth.

13. See Robert Grams Hunter, *Shakespeare and the Comedy of Forgiveness* (New York, 1965), pp. 157–158.

experience received by Midas. It is still a hybrid if we enlarge our context to the Elizabethan romantic drama surrounding Lyly's career. That rather breathless romance of the early 1580s, *The Rare Triumphs of Love and Fortune*, presents a human story purely as the fallout from a divine dispute. Twenty-five years later, *Pericles* focuses upon the human achievement of patience, Diana appearing only to crown the end. In the former, human activity is mere exemplum; in the latter divine appearance is mere reward. Lyly wishes us to see both the human struggle and the divine revelation. The result may sound peculiar, an uneasy compromise, and indeed I can cite no other play as parallel. But the circumstances of performance were unusual. As Hunter has well argued, no other dramatist created plays that both paid homage to the queen and yet retained artistic self-sufficiency. The parallel for *Endimion* lies outside the drama, the parallel of Spenser. *The Faerie Queene* presents both the human quest and the virtues that are its goal, both the narrative and the glowing allegorical visions central to each book. The enormous differences of style between Lyly's light, mannerist acrobatics and Spenser's serious, passionate questing, resulting from enormous differences in temperament and genre, should not, I think, conceal the basic similarity of idea and the fundamental likeness of dynamic, the extraordinarily economical dynamic of allegory that can encompass both our human struggles and our divine goals. *Endimion* is Lyly's Legend of Constancie.

IV

I should like to close with a mildly polemical coda. An old critical dispute about romance is once again heating up. In their recent books on Shakespearean romance, both Hallett Smith and Howard Felperin stress the specifically human experience in Shakespeare's last plays, Smith pointing out many resemblances between the late plays and Shakespeare's earlier work, and Felperin facing directly the question whether romance is escapist.[14] Almost inevitably, both books contain appendices disparaging allegorists and mythmongers. In this controversy I find myself between the armies.

It is easy to attack doctrinal and psychological allegorists; their

14. Hallet Smith, *Shakespeare's Romances* (San Marino, Calif., 1972), and Howard Felperin, *Shakespearean Romance* (Princeton, 1972).

interpretations usually err on the side of over-elaboration and rigidity. I cannot find that either Lyly or Shakespeare embodies within plays entire philosophical systems, let alone Christological allegories. A diffused, generalized Christian Neoplatonism provides Lyly with an occasional image or an occasional idea, but deft as he is in artistic structure, he is no systematic thinker. I will also join Professor Felperin in regretting the more extreme moments in twentieth-century criticism when all particulars of text and history have vanished into religious experience or synchronic myth. But since the tide now appears to be flowing in the opposite direction, since a secular scepticism now appears to be a prominent critical touchstone, I find the present battle more acute on the other side. Professor Felperin's book is the product of bright perception, and I applaud his attempt to refute the charge that romance and romantic vision are escapist, but in the refutation he gives away far too much to those who bring the charge. Discussing Shakespeare's emphasis upon quotidian reality, he cites the wrinkles of the resurrected Hermione:

> Devouring time is transcended even as its power is acknowledged. . . .
> A lesser romancer than Shakespeare would have produced an un-
> wrinkled Hermione, as Lyly had produced an unwrinkled Endymion
> more than two decades earlier. In that old play, the presiding figure
> of Cynthia is numinous enough to revive the hero from his forty-year
> sleep, restore his lost youth with a kiss, transform [Bagoa] from a
> tree back to a maid, and even reform [Tellus], all without even
> breathing hard. This is such stuff as wish-dreams are made on, and
> Paulina and Prospero himself might well envy her success.[15]

About Shakespeare, Felperin is of course right. Even in the romance form, his characters are earthbound. Even when Jupiter assures Posthumus that all will be well, his riddling prophecies can be understood only after the mortal characters themselves have resolved their misunderstandings, a resolution entailing the painful, public self-degradation of Posthumus. We live in a world of human hopes and fears, even in a world of human scepticism, occasionally invited to "hoot" at the plot as at "an old tale." Felperin rightly acquits Shakespeare of escapism on the ground of

---

15. Felperin, *Shakespearean Romance*, p. 53. Cynthia's kiss, of course, only awakens Endimion; his youth is not restored until she grants him her special favour two scenes later.

his own literary technique and his strong ethical consciousness. But the argument further implies that romancers who are not earthbound, sceptical and pervasively ethical, romancers like Lyly, are deplorably escapist. Endimion's reward for constancy is a wish-dream. This is sadly limiting. One could defend Lyly on Felperin's own ground; Lyly is sufficiently self-critical to include a powerful streak of anti-idealism in his play. The anarchic page-boys of *Endimion* mock their masters' devotion, produce cynical chop-logic on friendship, and together with Sir Tophas reduce love to eating, pure appetite. But Felperin's error is more fundamental. He would limit romance, or good romance, on a premise drawn from philosophical scepticism: use gods and Neoplatonic forms sparingly, and surround them with qualifications, for they are probably wish-dreams. The heart of his argument lies in a cogent passage he quotes from Harry Berger:

> Both [Neoplatonic idealism and Sidney's golden poetics] seem to presuppose a desire to move beyond the imperfections and unresolved tensions of actual life. "To move beyond," however, is an ambiguous phrase; does it mean, in any particular case, "to cope with and master," or "to escape from"? Is resolution achieved by true reconciliation, or by avoidance? Is the goal an ethical ideal (what *should* be) or a hedonist idyll (what *could* be)? It is tempting to construe a vision of the ideal or idyllic as a vision of the real. In the quest for God it may not always be easy to distinguish the urge to transcend oneself from the urge to get rid of oneself. The mind may visualize the condition to which it aspires as a perfect place – heaven, paradise, utopia, fairyland, arcadia – but this *locus amoenus* may be designed primarily as a mental hideout from one or another set of earthly imperfections.[16]

The sceptical rigour is admirable here, but sceptical rigour is a contemporary ideal, our current wisdom. These judgments are all prescriptive; they depend upon extra-literary axioms. One could turn Berger's argument on its head, saying it is equally tempting to cling to the earthly imperfections that we know, our old friends those unresolved tensions; for if embodied virtues and sacred places do exist, to encounter them might be terrifying. Cynthia is a difficult queen to serve.

16. Harry Berger, "The Renaissance Imagination: Second World and Green World," *Centennial Review*, IX (1965), 40.

Such philosophical dispute is perhaps remote from the playful and self-deprecating grace with which Lyly handles his courtly legend of constancy. He aimed only at delight. But if we would see what things could give delight in the 1580s, we had better reckon with the idealism of that age, however delicately a courtier might handle it. Lyly does not create dramatic embodiments of whole philosophical systems. But neither (except in *Campaspe* and *Mother Bombie*, his only plays without gods) does he stay earthbound in imperfections and mere ethics. In a realm between, he presents a handful of qualities: constancy in *Endimion*, love and chastity in the pastoral plays. Usually he is content to display and explore these qualities, to remind us that they are and what they are, to cause us to delight in them. In *Endimion* there is some increase in moral pressure, perhaps because of the quality concerned (there is a sense in which love simply happens but constancy must be achieved), perhaps because of the importance of that quality in Lyly's milieu (constancy is the vital heart of the relationship between courtier and queen). But preeminently these qualities are seen as universals, radiating through human life with more than human power, and therefore suitably imaged by the divinities who stand in the centre of his plays. Despite our secular scepticism, no one has yet proved that there is no reality corresponding to such images, or that such a reality, if it exists, is unapproachable by human beings. If some one does, we may lose touch with important experiences in both life and literature: wonder, enlargement beyond the quotidian, the possibility of an unquestioned devotion.

The Staging of
The Spanish Tragedy

D. F. ROWAN

"Hieronimo, Hieronimo; Oh let me see Hieronimo acted." Scholars have not been quick to echo William Prynne's account of a "late English Gentlewoman of good ranke; who daily bestowing the expense of her best houres upon the stage," closed her dying eyes crying for one more glimpse of the Knight Marshall of Spain going about his deadly business.[1] I doubt if it has been the force of Prynne's impassioned exhortation which has dissuaded them from wasting their "best houres" on the study of the Elizabethan stage and Elizabethan staging; rather, I suspect it has been the uncertain and dubious nature of our understanding of what Greg once characterized as "a misty mid region of Weir." It is only within the last decade that our knowledge of the physical structure of the Elizabethan theatre has become solid enough to serve as a foundation for anything but the most adventitious essays in reconstruction of actual stage presentations. Even yet the problems presented by certain plays are capable of only the most speculative solutions, and *The Spanish Tragedy* is such a play. Unlike Hieronimo, who uses his little play as a stalking horse for bigger game, I must content myself with using this great but puzzling play to start only a few small hares.

It is scarcely necessary to document the popularity of this play in an attempt to demonstrate its central and commanding position in a study of Elizabethan staging. Professor Jean Fuzier's detailed analysis of the evidence in Henslowe's diary reveals that for the

1. William Prynne, *Histriomastix* (1633), fol. 556ᵇ.

period from early 1592 until late 1597 it was the third most popular play, being presented twenty-nine times, against thirty-six times for *The Jew of Malta* and thirty-two times for the unhappily lost *The Wise Man of West Chester*. *Dr. Faustus* was mounted twenty-five times in the same period.[2] Although direct evidence is lacking, there is reason for believing that by 1592 it was already an old favourite, and it may well have continued in the repertoire until the closing of the theatres in 1642. The succession of ten or eleven editions from the 1590s to the last quarto of 1633 – the corrected, amended and enlarged edition of 1602, and the series of illustrated quartos beginning in 1615 – all testify to its vitality. Its popularity is further amply confirmed by the astonishing number of allusions to the play by Kyd's contemporaries and successors. Professor Claude Dudrap offers one hundred and eleven citations, ranging from Nashe's vitriolic attack in 1589 to Shirley's *The Constant Maid* of 1640, and goes on to argue most persuasively that *The Spanish Tragedy* probably never totally disappeared from the public theatres of London during the Jacobean and Caroline period.[3] The play was carried abroad to Germany and the Low Countries, and it was equally popular in the provinces of England when the actors took to the road. Jonson is taunted in Dekker's *Satiromastix* (1602) with making one of a pack of strolling players.

Thou hast forgot how thou amblest (in leather pilch) by a play wagon, in the high way, and tooks't mad Ieronimoes part, to get service among the Mimickes. (IV.i.130–2)

I need labour an obvious point no further, but conclude by stating that *The Spanish Tragedy* was mounted on a wide variety of temporary and permanent stages over a period of at least fifty years.

There is direct evidence for the staging of the play at the Rose theatre in the period from 1592 to 1597. As a property of Strange's Men it could have been acted as well at the Cross Keys Inn, The Theatre and at Newington Butts. As an Admiral's play it was certainly acted at the Fortune, and again possibly at The Theatre and Newington Butts. There is some evidence – centred on Richard

2. Jean Fuzier, "Carrière et Popularité de la *Tragédie Espagnole* en Angleterre," *Dramaturgie et Société*, ed. Jean Jacquot (1968), II, 589–606.
3. Claude Dudrap, "La *Tragédie Espagnole* Face à la Critique Élizabéthaine et Jacobéenne," *Dramaturgie et Société*, II, 607–631.

Burbage in the role of Hieronimo – to associate the play with the Chamberlain/King's Men. If this evidence, suggesting multiple auspices for the play, be accepted, then the Curtain, the First Globe and possibly the Second Blackfriars can be added to the list. Arthur Freeman concludes his admirable survey of the evidence of production by remarking that "we have evidence of productions of Kyd's play by no less than four companies between 1592 and 1604." He notes as well that "it must also be remembered that *The Spanish Tragedy* was in print, and the City companies would have little power to inhibit provincial players from using the book."[4] As always, the unhappy Swan perches aloof, although Pembroke's men fresh from the Swan opened their brief stay at the Rose on 11 October 1597 with a production of *The Spanish Tragedy*. One might be tempted to add – "direct from its signal success at Paris Garden." Be that as it may, my intent is, I am sure, clear at this point. Some productions of *The Spanish Tragedy* must have been mounted on the barest of scaffolds with perhaps only a traverse at the back, while others were presented on permanent stages with trapdoors, backed by two- or three-door tiring-house facade, and topped with an upper acting area.

At this point I have perhaps succeeded in destroying whatever validity my original thesis may have had. Can one usefully talk in general terms about "The Staging of *The Spanish Tragedy*"? I believe not; the topic is too large and the unknowns too numerous. Given the uncertain nature of the text and the unknown structure of a variety of stages, the equation is capable of an indeterminate number of equally valid solutions. Although I am convinced that the professional theatres – public, private and courtly – constituted a continuum and offered essentially the same physical facilities, a flat stage with two or three doors at the back, and an "above" and a "below," the best that one can offer is the tentative conclusion that it *might* have been done in such a way, or that it *could* have been presented in this manner.

But such indeterminate solutions are unsatisfying, and theatrical scholars are loath to rest content in an unstable condition. Many have pressed the evidence too far, uncritically rejecting, accepting, adding, selecting and rearranging the stage directions and portions of the text to yield a positive result; such is the case with Irwin

4. Arthur Freeman, *Thomas Kyd: Facts and Problems* (Oxford, 1967), p. 125.

Smith's *Shakespeare's Blackfriars Playhouse* (1964). The early sections of this study are models of scholarly enquiry, but the final half of the book is vitiated by the uncritical use of the evidence of stage directions. Perhaps still more culpable (if that is not too strong a term) is the work of scholars who have solved their equation by the creation of a physical facility for which there is no evidence, other than their own speculation. Such a work is John Cranford Adams' *The Globe Playhouse* of 1942. His full-blown "inner Stage" – the baseless fabric of a vision – still haunts all who teach Elizabethan drama.

We have yet to learn the lesson that we must not tamper with the evidence, unsatisfactory though it may be, nor create out of whole cloth a pat solution to a puzzling problem. In a recent note in *English Studies* it is suggested that some inconvenient stage directions in *The Spanish Tragedy* be reversed.

It is of course more natural for the murderers first to fall on Horatio and stab him – "thus, and thus" – and then hang his body in the arbour. . . . So I respectfully move that in future editions the two stage directions *They hang him in the arbour* and *They stab him* change places, reminding my readers how often and how easily stage directions were misplaced in Elizabethan and Jacobean plays.[5]

I am glad to report that such complacency did not go unchallenged, but elicited a sharp rebuttal.[6] Even more disheartening is the unbridled speculation offered by Freeman in his discussion of the staging of the bloody climax of the play.

It may indeed be that the initial breaking in and holding of Hieronimo is done by attendants or guards, entering from off-stage, but the rest must arrive there, too, and the quicker the better. May one conjecture a struggle long enough to allow the others time to descend? [Clearly the right answer!] Or additional steps, possibly for this occasion only, leading from the gallery directly to the stage? I would myself prefer to imagine a rather long piece of physical action . . . involving attendants from off-stage, the unlocking or breaking of a door between gallery and a short curved staircase – like an Elizabethan

5. Claes Schaar, "They hang him in the arbor," *English Studies*, 47 (1966), 27–28.
6. James L. Smith, "They hang him in the arbor," *English Studies*, 47 (1966), 372–373.

pulpit's – to the stage, with the pell-mell descent of the observers following.[7]

Freeman's suggestion of a short curved staircase is symptomatic. A careful scholar who has written a useful and responsible study of Kyd, he does not scruple to play fast and loose with the Elizabethan stage itself. There is no evidence for a visible staircase in the Elizabethan theatre.

Those scholars and editors who, in their recent editions, have avoided a direct discussion of the staging of this play have perhaps been wisely circumspect.[8] *The Spanish Tragedy* presents a wide array of other problems, many of which are more susceptible to satisfying solutions. The problems of authorship and date, texts and additions, themes and structure, language and imagery have all received due attention and yielded modest scholarly rewards. Nevertheless, despite the dangers already rehearsed and in a most tentative spirit of enquiry with a number of caveats clamouring in our ears, we might venture to look directly at the evidence of stage production.

Like *Soliman and Perseda* – attributed to Kyd partly on the grounds of style, and partly because the plot is an elaboration of "the play within the play" – *The Spanish Tragedy* presents a number of intriguing theatrical problems. Although it has no "Enter Basilisco riding on a Mule" or "Piston getteth up on his Asse, and rideth with him to the door, and meeteth the Cryer" both plays make use of allegorical figures. Love, Fortune and Death introduce *Soliman and Perseda*, after which they exit to reappear at the end of each act with the specific stage direction "Enter Chorus." It is clear that they leave the stage from the stage directions and such comments as:

> Why stay we then, lets give the Actors leave,
> And as occasion serves, make our returne.[9]

They remain aloof from the action, only returning to moralize the tragedies of each preceding act. The Ghost of Andrea and the

7. Freeman, *Thomas Kyd*, p. 114.
8. For example, Philip Edwards for "The Revels Plays" in 1959 (reprinted 1965), or Andrew S. Cairncross for "The Regents Renaissance Drama Series" in 1967.
9. *Soliman and Perseda* [1599], A2^v.

Spirit of Revenge are much more central to the theme, action and structure of *The Spanish Tragedy* and their deeper involvement is reflected in the fact that they remain in sight of the audience or as part of the audience throughout the play. With much trepidation I suggest that the disturbing entries at the end of the third and fourth acts – Enter Ghost and Revenge – may simply indicate a coming to centre stage to introduce "a dumme shew" at the end of the third act, and to formally close the play at the end of the fourth act.[10]

In keeping with my understanding of their function in the play I would not place them "above" but somewhere on the main stage where they may the more easily discharge their double roles as presenters and beholders of the tragic spectacle. In passing I might note that such staging may offer a clue to the interpretation of the much disputed paragraph of invective in Thomas Nashe's preface to Robert Greene's *Menaphon* (1589). At the end of the play the Ghost of Andrea and Revenge presumably exit as they entered. Revenge opens his final speech thus: "Then haste we downe to meet thy freends and foes" (L2ᵛ). I suggest that they exit through a trap (or even over the side of a temporary stage) just as they entered at the beginning of the play. Andrea's opening speech makes it clear that he and Revenge have come directly from Pluto's classical realm and yet they have presumably just entered from beneath the stage, the traditional theatrical "Hell." Perhaps this lends an edge to Nashe's otherwise seemingly unfounded charge that Kyd was one of those "that thrust Elisium into Hell . . ."[11]

From Hell to the Earthly Paradise is one short step on the Elizabethan stage.

> Come Bel-imperia let us to the bower,
> And there in safetie pass a pleasant hower. (D2)

With Horatio I invite you to the poetic "bower," or the more pedestrian "arbor," as it is distinguished in the two supporting stage directions. We cannot linger the promised "pleasant hower," but the "bower" demands our attention as the focus of the central problem in the staging of the play.

10. My basic text is the Scholar Press reproduction of the quarto of [1592]. All quotations are from this reproduction. (See note 13.)
11. For an excellent summary of this whole question once again see Freeman, *Thomas Kyd*, pp. 39–48.

If we are sympathetic to an emblematic theory of Elizabethan stage practice then the bower must be as central theatrically as it is thematically, its physical presence visually reinforcing the dramatic ironies of a "bower of blisse" becoming a "bower of death," a garden of earthly delights becoming a charnel house.

The "bower" and the "arbor" of *The Spanish Tragedy* present in an illuminating way a central problem of the examination of Elizabethan staging, the use of properties. The texts of many Elizabethan plays appear to offer firm evidence of certain physical features of the stage or theatre. The Prologue to *Henry V* may throw much light on the shape of the Globe theatre. But is Shakespeare speaking precisely or only generally when he speaks of a "Wooden O"?

Often the evidence of the text is capable of only poetic interpretation, as when Cassius bids Pindarus to "get higher on that hill." We know that there could not have been an actual hill, so we assume, with the support of the text which reads "Pind. Above," that he has simply moved to the upper acting area; a situation similar to that when "Pedringano sheweth all to the Prince and Lorenzo, placing them in secret." The staging is made clear by the subsequent stage direction, "Balthazar above." (This complex of directions is an excellent example of a "theatrical" direction supplementing and complementing an "authorial" direction.)

The problem of interpretation is not critical when the text speaks of relatively massive physical features such as hills, mountains or cliffs which were surely not in the company's chest of theatrical properties; it is when the dramatist writes of windows, banks, trees, towers, gates, walls and bowers – features which could conceivably have been more or less realistically represented on the stage that the vexing question presents itself in its most difficult form.

Most often the evidence is not capable of certain interpretation, and preconceptions of what the stage *may* have been like interfere with judicious assessment. How is one to interpret the evidence of the text in a speech such as Romeo's hymn to Juliet?

> But soft, what light through yonder window breaks?
> It is the East, and Juliet is the Sunne.

Was it a real light? Was it a real window? I suspect that Juliet enters with a candle or lamp in the upper acting area but there is no window, nor do I believe that a real window is required by the "authorial" direction "Bel-imperia at a window."

Not only is the authentic evidence of the primary texts difficult to assess, but meddling editors of the past, seeking to help the reader by expanding the stage directions, have complicated the problem for those who wish to visualize the Elizabethan stage as it really was. On the basis of a *single* quarto and folio direction, and on the text, the direction "Enter Romeo alone" becomes:

Scene I. A lane by the wall of Capulet's orchard. He climbs the wall, and leaps down within it. Juliet appears above at a window.

The wall over which Romeo leaps is built of bricks from the text.

He ran this way and leapt this Orchard wall.

.   .   .   .

The Orchard walls are high, and hard to climbe.

.   .   .   .

With Loves light wings/did I ore-perch these walls.

Often when the evidence of the text for real bricks seems most clear and certain, it is precisely then that the evidence is most doubtful. The dramatist builds with language a property which did not exist on the stage.[12]

The evidence of *The Spanish Tragedy* fortunately does not leave us in doubt about the "real presence" of Horatio's "fathers pleasant bower." There is a bower in which the lovers can sit – or lie – and in which the body of Horatio can be hanged. Happily the poetic, leafy bower of the author's dramatic imagination is supported by the more pedestrian and practicable stage directions: "They hang him in the Arbor." and "She cuts downe the Arbour."

The *O.E.D.* offers some comfort to the proponents of the "inner stage" in one meaning of the word "bower": "2. An inner apartment, esp. as distinguished from the 'hall,' or large public room, in ancient mansions." However it is the third meaning which is clearly apposite to our purpose: "3. A place closed in or over-arched with branches of trees, shrubs, or other plants; a shady

12. An elegant and sensitive discussion of this question is found elsewhere in this volume: Inga-Stina Ewbank, " 'What words, what looks, what wonders?': Language and Spectacle in the Theatre of George Peele," pp. 124–154.

recess, leafy covert, arbour." For "arbour" we read: "5. A bower or shady retreat, of which the sides and roof are formed by trees and shrubs closely planted or intertwined, or of lattice-work covered with climbing shrubs and plants."

Although illustrative or decorative woodcuts in early books are notoriously unreliable, the evidence of the frontispiece of the 1615 quarto, in conjunction with the evidence of the text and the stage directions, is incontrovertible. There was a property arbour on stage, and the pertinent questions are whether it remained on stage throughout the play, and where it was located on the stage. I am convinced that it remained on stage from first to last, an emblem of the womb of destiny, of life and death. Probably placed against the back wall when not in use, it was brought forward to the forestage when needed; the same stage attendants who bring in the banquet of Act I easily moving the light structure downstage and up.

Whether this same arbour serves as the stake to which Alexandro is bound and as the gallows on which Pedringano is "turned off" I cannot say. Stakes, if not gallows, are common enough on the Elizabethan stage and the staging of these episodes should present no insurmountable problems, even to an ill-equipped wandering troupe. The most challenging of problems is the mounting of the "play within the play" and the staging of the catastrophic final act.

The problem of the "discovery" of the dead body of Horatio has always perplexed me. Hieronimo in an earlier speech has promised a grande finale.

> . . . for the conclusion
> Shall prooue the inuention, and all was good:
> And I my selfe in an Oration,
> And with a strange and wonderous shew besides
> That I will have there behinde a curtaine,
> Assure your selfe shall make the matter knowen.
> And all shall be concluded in one Scene, . . .[13]

It would be dramatically and thematically effective to reveal the body of Horatio hanging in the arbour as it was in the earlier scene in the play. If there is demonstrative force in Hieronimo's

13. I take this speech from the quarto of 1602 which corrects the obvious textual corruption of the earlier quarto [1592] which reverses the order of the fourth and fifth lines of the passage quoted. *Malone Society Reprints* (1925), ll. 2849–2855.

"there" – "That I will have *there* behind a curtain" – he gestures toward the empty on-stage arbour. He exits and the lunatic Isabella enters "with a weapon" to hew down the very bower in which Horatio died. "She cuts downe the Arbour" or rather hacks away at the branches, boughs, blossoms and leaves which cover the arbour, ending her attack with:

> And with this weapon will I wound the brest,
> The haples brest that gaue Horatio sucke. (K2)

This is supported by the marginal stage direction "She stabs herself." She has no exit, but rather Hieronimo *immediately* enters: "*Enter Hieronimo, he knocks vp the curtaine.*" *The* curtain, presumably, promised in his earlier prologue.

I have never been convinced by Richard Hosley's argument, accepted by P. W. Edwards in the Revels Edition of 1959, that the Spanish King and his court do not sit "above" to witness the play within the play. Hieronimo's speech to the Duke of Castile is central to the argument.

> Let me intreat your grace
> That when the traine are past into the gallerie,
> You would vouchsafe to throwe me downe the key. (K2^v)

I quote from the relevant Revels Edition note.

> The gallery is not a balcony but the hall; it is clear from the action later, and (as Hosley points out) from Balthazar's bringing on a chair for the King (1.16) that the audience of the play-within-the-play is on the main stage with the actors. *throw me down the key* must therefore mean "throw the key down [on the floor] for me." (p. 110)

The scene could be acted in this manner, and no doubt was on temporary stages without an "above," but it is inconceivable to me that the upper acting area – a feature of every permanent theatre – should not be used. The King of Spain and his court sit isolated above the tiring-house wall, locked in by the tiring-house doors, pathetic in their impotence as Hieronimo plays out his bloody charade.

And yet how is the body of Horatio to be hanged in the arbour in full view of the audiences, both real and dramatic? It is clear that the arbour must be set against the tiring-house wall, backed against one of the doors through which the "dead" body can enter. Hieronimo when "he knocks up the curtain" must cover the arbour with a cloth. I must again quote the relevant Revels note:

> It is difficult to judge what precisely Hieronimo does. (i) What is involved in 'knocking up' a curtain? Probably a hasty hanging of a curtain in a prepared place. (ii) Where was the curtain? The best suggestion is that it hung over one of the doors, so that Horatio's body could conveniently be brought behind it. (p. 110)

If then the arbour covered with the curtain must be placed against the back wall so that it can load its deadly freight the courtly audience "above" cannot see Hieronimo's gruesome revelation.

> I see your lookes urge instance of these words,
> Beholde the reason vrging me to this.
> *Shewes his dead sonne.*
> See heere my shew, look on this spectacle: (K4)

Hosley and Edwards must be correct and despite the contrary evidence the court must be sitting on the main stage. Either that, or the arbour after loading must be brought forward from the back wall so that it can be seen from "above."

In my frustration in attempting to solve the riddle of Horatio's dead body I even toyed with the idea of using a painting – perhaps the painting done by the painter of the fourth addition of 1602 – concealed within the arbour. But this will not do. The solution is far simpler, and solves as well a related problem presented by the text of this prickly play. The answer is found in an old theatrical trick rooted deeply in the conventions of medieval and early Tudor drama.

Many editors have noted the absence of an "exit" for Isabella, or of any attempt to remove her dead body after her suicide.[14] All have assumed that she staggers off-stage to die, and that the "exit" is accidentally omitted from a text which is otherwise remarkably careful in getting characters off the stage. But the omission of the "exit" is not accidental; indeed it is the clue which solves the riddle. The arbour is placed on the fore-stage for Isabella's attack and suicide. It dominates the scene and she enters the arbour to destroy it, stabs herself, sinks to the floor and dies within the arbour. Hieronimo *immediately* enters and "knocks up the curtain" covering the arbour and the body. The actor playing Isabella, the mother, is resurrected into the dead body of Horatio, a metamorphosis theatrically striking and thematically satisfying. The Spanish court sits above; the emblematic arbour remains in the centre of the stage, clearly visible to all, shrouded, threatening, freighted with death and promising still further carnage. A simple and conventional doubling and the staging of the final act becomes a thematic and theatrical tour de force.

Harkening to my own introductory remarks I cannot nor would not claim that this is the only way in which this play could or would be staged. So popular a play mounted by such a wide variety of companies on so many different stages cannot be constrained to one – and only one – form of presentation; but I am convinced that this is the way that it was acted at the Rose on Bankside. I only hope that I shall not have to imitate old Hieronimo and bite out my tongue.

14. See Edwards' note on page 109 of the Revels Edition.

"What words, what looks, what wonders?":
Language and Spectacle in the Theatre of George Peele

INGA-STINA EWBANK

The title of this paper contains one of the more unrecognizable quotations of the conference; but I take heart when I am asked (as I have been) whether it refers to Shakespeare's Marina, or to T. S. Eliot's.[1] Such guesses help to confirm my feeling that there is, at times, in the theatrical art of George Peele a peculiar quality of wonder and, though that is not my main concern, that this makes him very occasionally anticipate certain Shakespearian moments. This "wonder" – Peele's version of *admiratio*[2] – is, I believe, produced by some notable combinations of visual and verbal effects. The quotation, then, is offered as a paradigm of the quest I propose: for it is a quest, rather than a thesis, and the most important part of the quotation is the question mark. What is the relationship between language and spectacle in the theatre of Peele?

1. I should point out that the quotation has been slightly tailored to suit the paper. Line 49 in *David and Bethsabe* reads: "What tunes, what words, what looks, what wonders pierce . . ."; but, as I cannot attempt to deal with the contribution made by music to the total theatrical effect, I have cut out the "tunes." All quotations from Peele are taken from the three volumes of *The Dramatic Works of George Peele*, general editor Charles Tyler Prouty (New Haven, Conn., 1952, 1961 and 1970).

2. For a discussion of Renaissance theory and practice of *admiratio*, see J. V. Cunningham, *Woe or Wonder: The Emotional Effect of Shakespearean Tragedy* (Denver, Colorado, 1951), esp. chapter IV.

Though this conference has dealt chiefly with issues of pre-Shakespearian stage history and stage conditions, I feel by now no need to apologize – as for a feminine ending to the mighty line of the other papers – for closing it with an apparently literary paper. For the proceedings of the conference have also made it clear that, whether we call ourselves theatre historians or dramatic scholars or literary critics, we are all deeply dependent on each other's work. And this, of course, only reflects the interdependence of the means whereby the theatre works. From the audience's point of view the basic interdependence is that of their own senses:

> The unique distinction of drama as an Art is that it appeals to eye and ear simultaneously. The emotions of the recipient are open to assault through two senses at once and, as his emotional temperature rises, the auditor-spectator has the focal length of his imagination steadily enlarged to a point where the mind may perceive truth, meaning, reality, unobtainable by processes of the intellect alone.[3]

There is an almost Wordsworthian sense of "something far more deeply interfused" in this passage which no doubt has to do with the fact that Professor Wickham is trying to account for the birth of drama out of the liturgy of the Christian church. But it also has to do, I think, with the fact that at the heart of all living theatrical experience there is a kind of mystery: a creation, through what we see and hear, of a world which we accept as possible.[4] We may, in Hippolita's words, see what is presented to us as "strange and admirable," but we also share her readiness to accept it as "something of great constancy." Situations of wonder offer an extreme form of such experience. Extreme, because they tend to present characters who themselves experience extremes of feeling: not only joy but also grief or horror; Macbeth as well as Miranda speaks of being rapt with "wonder." Extreme, too, because they involve a particularly keen sense of the possible *and* the impossible, best described by Pericles when he tells Marina

> I will believe thee,
> And make my senses credit thy relation
> To points that seem impossible. (V.i.121–3)

3. Glynne Wickham, *Early English Stages*, I (London, 1959), C310.
4. "Possible" seems to me a more adequate word in this context than "real," with its misleading associations of "suspension of disbelief."

Inga-Stina Ewbank

The experience of the impossible becoming possible is obviously
central to Shakespeare's last plays: felt most keenly, perhaps, in
the wordless wonder of the last scene of *The Winter's Tale* and
described most fully in the penultimate scene of the same play:

> . . . the changes I perceived in the King and Camillo were *very notes
> of admiration*. They seem'd almost, with staring on one another, to
> tear the cases of their eyes; *there was speech in their dumbness,
> language in their very gesture; they look'd as they had heard of a
> world ransom'd, or one destroyed*. A notable passion of wonder ap-
> peared in them; but the wisest beholder that knew no more but seeing
> could not say if th' importance were *joy or sorrow* – but *in the ex-
> tremity of one* it must needs be. . . . This news, which is call'd true,
> is so like an old tale that the verity of it is in strong suspicion.
> (V.ii.9–29)

It is also central to the beginning of post-classical theatre: the
wonder of the three Marys discovering that Christ is not in the
tomb, or the wonder of the shepherds at the Nativity. Here, too,
it is a matter of an interaction between what we see and what we
hear, what the "playwright" shows and what he says. "*Venite, et
videte locum,*" the Angel urges the wondering women; and, before
they can articulate their joy in the anthem "*Surrexit Dominus de
sepulchre,/Qui pro nobis perpendit in ligno,*" the wonder must be
visually dramatized:

> *Hec vero dicens, surgat, et erigat velum, ostendatque eis locum cruce
> nudatum, sed tantum linteamina posita quibus crux involuta erat.*[5]

The lifting of the veil, or the "discovery," or the drawing of a
curtain which (as we shall see) marks the beginning and the end
of Peele's *David and Bethsabe*, is, either literally or metaphoric-
ally, as much part of the experience of wonder as is the verbal
articulation of extreme states: things dying and things new-born,
or things transfigured by passion as in Belimperia's plea

> O let me goe, for in my troubled eyes,
> Now maist thou read that life in passion dies.
> (*The Spanish Tragedy*, II.iv.47–8)

5. From the *Regularis Concordia* of Ethelwold, usually assigned to the year
967. Quoted from John M. Manly, *Specimens of the Pre-Shakespearean
Drama*, I (Dover Publications reprint, N.Y., 1967), p. xx.

Because of our unfamiliarity with most pre-Shakespearian plays on stage, we tend to underestimate their theatrical *life*, as against such verbal patternings and spectacular arrangements as we can easily apprehend from the texts in front of us. In the summer of 1973, undergraduates at London University still believe that Horatio and Belimperia go into the arbour for the express purpose of having stychomythia.[6] The men writing for the London theatres in the 1580s and early 1590s were particularly strongly subjected to pulls in two directions: towards the word, in the shape of exuberant and/or horrific rhetoric, and towards spectacle in every sense, from the significant grouping to the bloody banquet or the coronation pageant. They responded, not with the schizophrenia of contemporary British theatre, but with a happy eclecticism. Renaissance scholarship is increasingly emphasizing that this was a period good at simultaneously entertaining apparently contradictory impulses; and nowhere, perhaps, do we see this more clearly than in the theatre. It is not only that a playwright like Peele could both compose the delicate lyric which opens *David and Bethsabe* and devise a dumb-show which needed "3. violls of blood and a sheeps gather",[7] but that he and his contemporaries were always trying out new ways of combining word and spectacle.

For such combination we are still quite short of a critical language and therefore, as the two are related like the chicken and the egg, of a sympathetic understanding. Anything short of the mature Shakespearian interaction of visual and verbal poetry tends too readily to be dismissed as spectacle decorated with verse or, at best, to be set down as a kind of emblematic art in which language and visual effects duplicate each other.[8] "That which can be made Explicit to the Idiot is not worth my care,"

6. Those who were lucky enough to see the production by the Other Theatre Company at the Mercury Theatre, London, in October 1973 (while this paper was being prepared for the press), will no longer think so; for the performance (despite – or because of – shoestring conditions) beautifully brought out the human reality underlying the patterned speeches.
7. See the theatrical plot of *The Battle of Alcazar*, in W. W. Greg, *Two Elizabethan Stage Abridgements* (Oxford, 1922), p. 32.
8. Dieter Mehl, "Visual and Rhetorical Imagery in Shakespeare's Plays," in *Essays and Studies* (1972), p. 95. Professor Mehl's is one of the few systematic attempts at discussing this subject. I have published a few thoughts on it in *Shakespeare Survey 24* (1971), 13–18 (" 'More Pregnantly than Words' ").

Blake says about such "Moral Painting";[9] and Peele and his contemporaries hardly saw their audiences as idiots. Though a great deal of dramatic language in this period does act mainly as commentary on tableaux, to stop at this point is to blinker oneself against the possibility of mutual illumination, of significant interaction, between "words" and "looks" which I wanted to hint at in my title quotation. It seems important, then, to ask questions about the relationship of word and show in the theatre immediately before Shakespeare. But perhaps the first question that springs to mind is whether Peele is an important enough playwright to ask such questions about? His theatrical career, in its variety of genres and audiences, seems largely opportunistic, lacking in the kind of inner compulsion which lies behind the work of Marlowe, and even Kyd. Therefore he has seemed, on the whole, unworthy of serious scholarly or critical study (always excepting the splendid Yale edition). Even those who have written on him have, in order not to appear to claim too much for him, leant over backwards so far as to make one wonder why they bother at all. In what follows, I shall err, if anything, on the side of generosity. In the theatre, I believe, there is room for an art which is mainly a search for what audiences need and want; and there is another kind of compulsion than an ideological-thematic one: a technical one, which involves the sheer pleasure of accomplishing certain effects in the theatre, doing certain things to audiences, being (in Emrys Jones' term)[10] a "technician of the emotions." It is to Peele as an eclectic technician of the emotions that I turn, in order to explore his words, looks and wonders.

My title quotation, of course, comes from the opening scene of *David and Bethsabe*. The *Prologus*, departing,

> *drawes a curtaine, and discovers Bethsabe with her maid bathing over a spring: she sings, and David sits above vewing her.*

At this point, what the audience is viewing is a tableau with familiar bearings. The motif of Bethsabe in the bath, from its frequent use in medieval Books of Hours to a number of sixteenth-century paintings, had become an image of earthly beauty, usually

9. Letter to the Revd. Dr. Trusler, August 23, 1799 (Nonesuch *Blake*, 4th ed., London, 1967, pp. 834–5).
10. *Scenic Form in Shakespeare* (Oxford, 1971).

with the connotations of moral condemnation.[11] But iconographical familiarity does not make the visual image self-sufficient, any more than a dumb-show of Cleopatra at Cydnus could substitute for Enobarbus' barge speech. The wonder of "the flower of Israel," as of the "rare Egyptian," comes in an appeal to all the senses, communicated through words – though Enobarbus' speech can create its own scene, while David's, like Iachimo's in Imogen's bedchamber, has the task, probably more precarious, of helping to convey something which the audience actually and simultaneously sees. What a literal-minded audience, of course, sees at the opening of *David and Bethsabe* (that is, what they saw in the 1590s), is a boy dressed up as a girl with, presumably, no more visual sex appeal than those sixteenth-century Dutch pictures of the bathing scene where Bethsabe is depicted as modestly washing her feet, her skirt pulled up to reveal at most her knees.[12] But Peele does not give the audience a chance to remain literal-minded: we "see" the scene through its words. First there is Bethsabe's song, the purely musical effect of which we cannot recapture, as the setting is lost. But the lyrical poem which remains creates a whole landscape of sensuousness, in which she herself is the focus:

> Hot sunne, coole fire, temperd with sweet aire,
> Black shade, fair nurse, shadow my white haire.
> Shine sun, burne fire, breathe aire, and ease mee,
> Black shade, fair nurse, shroud me and please me.
> Shadow (my sweet nurse) keep me from burning,
> Make not my glad cause, cause of mourning.
> Let not my beauties fire,
> Enflame unstaied desire,
> Nor pierce any bright eye,
> That wandreth lightly.

The challenge of the situation has touched Peele's verbal imagination to particularly fine issues: the rhythm and the patterning give simple words a haunting suggestiveness far beyond their normal reach, and the total effect, rather than merely descriptive or celebratory, is of an awareness, as in a metaphysical poem, of

---

11. See my essay on "The House of David in Renaissance Drama," *Renaissance Drama*, VIII (1965), 3–40.
12. Ibid.. p. 13; and see Elisabeth Kunoth-Leifels, *Über die Darstellungen der "Bathseba im Bade": Studien zur Geschichte des Bildthemas 4. bis 17. Jahrhundert* (Essen, 1962).

many worlds.[13] One shudders to think that when William Poel revived *David and Bethsabe* in 1932, he told the actress who took the part of Bethsabe to compose her own song and enter singing any words she fancied.[14]

Then Bethsabe speaks, and in her invocation to Zephyr sensuousness changes into a Narcissistic sensuality which yet is so delicately balanced with innocence that no simplistic response is possible. Fair Bethsabe projects the wonder of irresistible physical beauty; we watch David watching her and having his whole consciousness pierced by the wonder:

> What tunes, what words, what looks, what wonders pierce
> My soule, incensed with a sudden fire?

Later in the play, David is going to look back on this scene and see it, as the illustrators of the Penitential Psalms did, as an emblem of concupiscence, sexual appetite. But within the dramatic present neither he nor the audience can take a coolly rational and moral view of the situation – any more than the scene in which Cleopatra helps to arm Antony could be circumscribed by the motto "The triple pillar of the world transform'd /Into a strumpet's fool." If Peele were a more respectable dramatist, we could use phrases like "visual and verbal ambivalence" about the climax of the scene, when David rhapsodizes in a rhetorical figure which itself enacts the whole sexual paradox,

> Bright Bethsabe gives earth to my desires,
> Verdure to earth and to that verdure flowers,
> To flowers, sweet Odors, and to Odors wings,
> That carrie pleasures to the hearts of Kings,

and when Bethsabe is brought up[15] to join him, elevated yet falling, representing both "earth" and "wings," flesh and spirit. As it is, we dare at least say that Peele's poetry feeds from the visual image and *vice versa*; and that he is making the theatre prove the wonder

13. Elizabeth Holmes, in *Aspects of Elizabethan Imagery* (Oxford, 1929), p. 16, draws attention to how "the quaint double suggestiveness of 'burning' catches even something of the metaphysical in its note."
14. See Robert Speaight, *William Poel and the Elizabethan Revival* (London, 1954), pp. 266–68.
15. Elmer Blistein, in his Yale edition of the play, believes that David *descends* to Bethsabe.

of being human and the impossibility of making simply moral responses to such wonder. David's experience, in so far as it involves having his soul "pierced" with "wonders," is by no means unique in Peele's drama. He likes to subject his characters to experiences which "pierce" or "daze" or "dazzle" them; and, indeed, both in his dramatic and his non-dramatic poetry there is much explicit interest in wonder: what it is and how it affects a beholder. Thus in *Anglorum Feriae*, the poem written to commemorate the Accession Day festivities of 1595, he declares his intention to

> recommende to Tymes Eternitie
> Hir [i.e. the Queen's] honors heigthe and woonders of hir age;
> Woonders of hir that reasons reache transcend,
> Suche woonders as hathe sett the Worlde at gaze; (ll. 13–6)

and in those wonders "that reasons reache transcend" lies the key to the dramatic structure of *The Arraignment of Paris* (as I shall presently argue). In *Edward I*, even the Queen Mother is overcome with the wonders of triumphant kingship. She opens the play with forty eloquent lines in which she envisages the return of her sons from their Holy Wars; but when she is faced with the actual pageant (carefully described for us in the stage directions), words fail her and "*she fals and sounds.*" In *The Arraignment of Paris* the shows of the three goddesses leave the protagonist in a daze which, like states of confusion in *Macbeth*, can only be articulated in a paradox:

> Most heavenly dames, was never man as I
> Poore shepherde swaine, so happy and unhappy; (ll. 509–10)

and (as, again, I shall presently argue) shows of the supernatural, "able" (in Paris' words) "to wrape and dazle humaine eyes," become in *The Battle of Alcazar* the device through which Peele tries to dramatize the wonder of extreme evil. For horror and evil have their wonders, too. Priam in Peele's *Tale of Troy*, like the mother of Edward I, is "mazde" by what he sees; but in the case of the unfortunate king it is "with frights and feares":

> Ah what a piercing sight it was to see,
> So fair a towne as Troy was said to be,
> By quenchlesse fire layd levell with the soyle. (ll. 424–6)

In all these examples, Peele is trying through words to communicate the effect of something seen. But sight is not the only sense involved in provoking an experience of wonder. In *The Honour of the Garter*, a poem apparently written to order, there is little excitement or evocativeness in the description of the garter procession as such; but where the poem comes alive is in the framework attempt to introduce that procession as a pageant in a dream. The wonder of the vision is rendered as an account of what used to be called "total theatre":

> Mine eyes, and eares, and senses all were served,
> With every object perfect in his kinde.
> And lo, a wonder to my senses all,
> For through the melting aire perfum'd with sweets,
> I might discerne a troope of Horse-men ride. . . . (ll. 34–8)

As in the *David and Bethsabe* passage which I have just been examining, Peele is interested in the whole banquet of sense; and this interest has a great deal to do with his qualities as a playwright.

One might have expected a young poet who had been at Oxford with neo-Latin dramatists like Richard Edes, Leonard Hutton and William Gager, to see drama primarily as a matter of verbal rhetoric. Nashe's praise of him as "the *Atlas* of Poetrie, and *primus verborum Artifex*" suggests that he was seen mainly as an artist in words.[16] But Christ Church had a theatrical tradition of spectacular entertainments; one remembers the cry of hounds in the quadrangle which so pleased the queen during the performance of Edwardes' *Palamon and Arcite* in 1566. And Peele himself, well after he had officially left Oxford, returned to stage-manage a scarcely less spectacular show put on before the visiting Polish Count Palatine, Alasco, in June 1583. This production of Gager's *Dido* contained the apparently indispensable hounds – "a goodlie sight of hunters with full crie of a kennell of hounds" – but it also involved such powerful appeals to various senses as

Mercurie and Iris descending and ascending from and to an high place, the tempest wherein it hailed small confects, rained rosewater,

16. *The Works of Thomas Nashe*, ed. R. B. McKerrow (London, 1904–10), III, 323.

and snew an artificiall kind of snow, all strange, marvellous, abundant.[17]

Similar appeals are involved in many of the pageant occasions, at court or in the city, with which Peele came to be connected during his post-Oxford career. The records which remain of these suggest that he tended to respond more to the occasion than to its intellectual or moral meaning. In *Polyhymnia*, for example, the versified description of the couples who tilted in the 1590 accession tournament, the strength of the verse lies in its rendering of the visual delight of costumes, armour, and so on; whereas the attempts at moral allegory are thin and perfunctory. The fact is, of course, that even a *primus verborum Artifex* held a very secondary position at such occasions. He may be showing his hand in Sir Henry Lee's farewell sonnet, "His golden lockes, Time hath to Silver turn'd" (if we may assume it to be by Peele), but it is worth remembering what a grand occasion it was a small part of. Sir William Segar's account of the way the Queen's Champion took his leave of her –

> Her Majesty beholding these armed Knights comming toward her, did suddenly heare a musicke so sweete and secret, as every one thereat greatly marveiled. And hearkening to that excellent melodie, the earth as it were opening, there appeared a Pavilion, made of white Taffata, containing eight score elles, being in proportion like unto the sacred Temple of the Virgin Vestall. This Temple seemed to consist upon pillars of Pourferry, arched like unto a Church, within it were many Lampes burning[18]

– suggests stage marvels like the last two scenes of *Pericles* rolled into one, while Peele's sonnet is introduced into this account simply as verses which "accompanied . . . the musicke aforesayd" and were "sung by M. *Hales* her Majesties servant, a Gentleman in that Arte excellent, and for his voice both commendable and admirable." The poet receives no mention and his art is clearly regarded as the handmaiden of the other arts.

The same is basically true for the Lord Mayor's pageants, though in the later of the two which have been preserved, *Descensus Astreae* (1591), the verbal images (the web and the fountain) are

17. Described by Holinshed (1587), quoted from *The Life and Minor Works of George Peele* (vol. 1 of the Yale edition), p. 61.
18. Ibid., p. 167.

more intrinsic to the show than any in the earlier *Pageant borne before Woolstone Dixi* (1585): a reflection, possibly, of Peele's experience of playwriting in the intervening years. By definition, obviously, a pageant poet's verses have to be functional: to explain as directly as possible to a wide and varied audience (many of whom would probably not hear the words anyway) what is seen, what it means and what "wonders" are being celebrated. If, as there is some evidence to suggest,[19] Peele was involved in producing pageants as well as writing for them, these functional needs would seem natural and no strait-jacket. It is worth pointing out, too, that the relationship works both ways; if the words are subordinated to a mainly visual situation, they are also themselves given meaning and weight by that situation. A couplet in *Descensus Astreae,*

> O let hir princely daies never have fine,
> Whose vertues are immortal and devine, (ll. 84–5)

is not particularly evocative or memorable on the page; but, spoken by the figure of one of those "vertues" (Charitie) in the company of other virtues and of Astrea, the manifestation of the queen's "devine" qualities, it must have had a very different resonance. As for "immortal," a spectator need only move his eyes to "the hinder part of the Pageant," where

> *did sit a Child, representing Nature, holding in her hand a distaffe, and spinning a Web, which was wheeled up by Time,*

and the conceit, of the queen's divine independence of ordinary human nature and time, would come alive – even more so if he remembered that the Presenter of the pageant spoke of how "Time and Kinde/Produce hir yeares to make them numberlesse" (ll. 33–4).

One wonders if the pageant writer's attitude to language – as something which does not so much evoke meanings and create patterns in its own right as *refer* to a visual reality, existing already, before the very eyes of the spectator – may not help to explain one feature of Peele's dramatic style that has often come under attack. I am thinking of his tendency to repeat the same, often colourless, adjective time and time again, a tendency decried as "monotony,

19. See D. M. Bergeron, *English Civic Pageantry, 1580–1642* (London, 1972).

poverty . . . emptiness and affectation."[20] For example, in the midst of the Coronation pageantry of *Edward I*, the queen appeals to the king in lines which, read at the scholar's desk, suggest the poor vocabulary of a modern teenager:

> And lovelie England to thy lovely Queene,
> Lovelie Queene Elinor, unto her turne thy eye,
> Whose honor cannot but love thee wel. (ll. 701–3)

Seen (and I use the verb advisedly) in context, the lines suggest a sense of decorum (little as we may like it): Peele is envisaging, rather than feeling into, the scene, and all the adjectives need do is to point to what the spectator can see: two "lovely" people in state, representing the honour and glory and growing unity of England.

I repeat that I am trying to explain, rather than excuse, what is often an irritating feature in Peele. But it is worth remembering how in the greatest moments of wonder in drama, language tends to take on this quality of simply referring to what is seen, as when the bystanders at Hermione's miraculous and silent reunion with Leontes speak only stage directions ("She embraces him," etc.). In *The Tempest* adjectives such as "strange" often function, like Peele's "lovely," merely as dotted lines on which he who has eyes to see and ears to hear may inscribe further meanings. And, of course, in the court masque proper the language often serves as a kind of incantatory pointer to what is seen. Jonson's *Vision of Delight* (1617) is, I think, the masque which most explicitly contemplates the wonder of its own devices (the main scene transformation into "the bower of Zephyrus," and the discovery of the main masquers as "the glories of the spring") as well as the wonder of monarchy. Ultimately the two wonders are fused: "Behold a king/Whose presence maketh this perpetual spring," and the choir turns what is seen into a litany of the King's power:

> The founts, the flowers, the birds, the bees,
> The herds, the flocks, the grass, the trees
> Do all confess him.

It is hardly necessary to point out how, outside the full context of the occasion, this reads merely like an inventory. It is written for

20. See John Dover Wilson's introduction to his New Shakespeare edition of *Titus Andronicus* (Cambridge, 1948), p. xxix.

spectators, to embody a delight

> Which who once saw would ever see;
> And if they could the object prize,
> Would, while it lasts, not think to rise,
> But wish their bodies all were eyes.[21]

Now, I do not for a moment think that in approaching a Peele play we wish our "bodies all were eyes." Even without Nashe's description of him, it is clear that Peele saw drama very much as a vehicle for poetry. There is the obvious delight in the writing itself: in experimenting (with metres in *The Arraignment of Paris*, with varieties of style and tone in *The Old Wives Tale*, with biblical and oriental imagery in *David and Bethsabe*) and in imitating fashionable modes (trying to out-Tamburlaine Tamburlaine in *The Battle of Alcazar* and to fit stretches of almost literal translations from Du Bartas into the texture of *David and Bethsabe*). There is also the evidence of at least one text, that of *The Arraignment of Paris*, that he was anxious for it to be read as literature in the strictest sense.[22] Notes are appended, like the critical guide to the dialogue between Thestilis and the shepherds: *"The grace of this song is in the Shepherds Ecco to her verse"* (1.742 SD); captions draw attention to the importance of the two big set speeches (Paris' to the Council of the Gods, and Diana's on – and to – Queen Elizabeth); and the poetic plums are marked out as if Peele had anticipated the coming of Lamb's *Specimen* (and indeed Colin's Lament and Oenone's Complaint both appeared in its 1600 equivalent, *England's Helicon*). But we must, to put this emphasis on the literary nature of the play in perspective, remember that it is an exceptional play, based entirely on the presence of the queen at performance.[23] To explain it, as the Yale

21. *Ben Jonson: The Complete Masques*, ed. Stephen Orgel (New Haven, Conn., 1969), pp. 253–54.
22. We are safe in seeing Peele's hand in the preparation of the text, as "the evidence concerning the printers' copy indicates that it was probably either the autograph manuscript or a careful transcript of it that served as the prompt book" (R. Mark Benbow, in his edition of *The Arraignment of Paris*, vol. 3 of the Yale edition, p. 57).
23. Peter Saccio, in *The Court Comedies of John Lyly* (Princeton, New Jersey, 1969), p. 16, n. 17, discusses the nonce-quality of the play and points out that it is unprofitable to speculate on the possible existence of an alternative version suitable for Blackfriars performance. For, "in any case, another version would have been a very different play."

editor does, by Peele's "conforming to the sixteenth-century conception that poetry but not drama was proper to the gentleman" is to forget that here is a play which as soon as the occasion (the first and probably only night) is gone, becomes "the book of the play." When no longer a play *to* and *for* the queen, it becomes a poem *about* her. And besides, even as a reading text the play testifies to the contrary pull, towards spectacle. The great care taken over the stage directions (and this applies to other Peele texts, too) helps to point to the fact that the words exist in visual situations. Sometimes those situations are as spectacular, and the dependence of the words on what is seen as incontestable, as in *The Vision of Delight*. "Lo," says Juno to Paris, "this Tree of Golde will I bestowe on thee." The stage direction tells us that *"hereupon did rise a Tree of gold laden with Diadems and Crownes of golde"*; whereupon Juno proceeds to put its wonders into words: "The body and the bark of golde, all glistringe to beholde," etc. But even in the less spectacular scenes there is an unusual directness of speech. A reference to visual actuality is often all we need: "Pomona with her fruite comes time enough I see" (1. 53), or "Pallas in flowers of hue and collowers read" (1. 110). As in a masque, there is little need for verbal conceit: the conceit lies in plot – or, rather, in structure, which here is plot. Again we must remember the exceptional nature of this play; with a mythological and a pastoral world actually presented on stage, verbal metaphors have resolved themselves into visual figurations before the play starts. There is some conventional Petrarchan imagery around the two unhappy lovers, Colin and Oenone. But even that becomes curiously literal when the stage also holds a character who can speak of *"Cupid* my sonne" as a matter of fact.

However exceptional, Peele's first play yet suggests that he saw himself as an *"artifex"* both in words and in shows. Returning, at last, to the point I started from, I feel that at key moments of "wonder" in his plays he achieves a kind of mutual illumination between his visual and his verbal imagery. I want now to turn to such moments in four of his plays. Time will not permit an examination of *The Old Wives Tale*, which is so much a thing in itself, though it is worth pointing out that the frame construction makes the whole of that play into one continuous "wonder" enacted before its stage audience.

I return to *The Arraignment of Paris* where, I believe, wonder is the point of the whole play. Usually it is seen as a work with an interesting middle – modern critics agreeing with Nashe about the "manifold variety of invention" displayed – but a misleading beginning and an unsatisfactory end. This is, of course, a very damning criticism; for if "this final episode in which Diana gives the apple to the Queen does not follow inevitably from what goes before,"[24] then not only the unity but also the entire *raison d'être* of the play will collapse. Two recent critics have attempted a defence in terms of the play's political and moral themes, both in the process moving on to "historico-mythical" levels which seem to me to have little to do with the reality of the play as a piece of theatre.[25] Andrew von Hendy finds "its spectacle, though plentiful, . . . relatively incidental" and so in fact undermines his own argument that the play "is constructed like a masque to induce the willing suspension of disbelief necessary to the compliment." But, it seems to me, if there is a unity in this gallimaufry of a play, it lies exactly in the spectacle; and if there is a suspension of disbelief, it comes not through rational argument about Britain as the new Troy or through allegorical correspondencies between Elizabeth and Christ, but through our being "dazed" with wonder, even as Paris was "dazed" by the shows presented before him. Even Ben Jonson had to admit that it was the outward show of the masque in performance which could "steal away the spectators from themselves";[26] and in *The Arraignment of Paris* it is Peele's sense of theatre that makes our senses credit the denouement "to points that seem impossible."

The wonder of the ending, in so far as we can paraphrase it in words, is the defeat of a whole tragic and dynamic world order (its dynamism having provided the action of the play) by the simple, static presence of the queen. Ate Prologus, who has been much maligned for misleading us, opens the play by establishing that order:

> So loath and weerie of her heavie loade
> The Earth complaynes unto the hellish prince,

24. G. K. Hunter, *John Lyly: The Humanist as Courtier* (London, 1962), p. 155.
25. Andrew von Hendy, "The Triumph of Chastity: Form and Meaning in *The Arraignment of Paris,*" *Renaissance Drama*, n.s. I (1968), 87–101: and Henry G. Lesnick, "The Structural Significance of Myth and Flattery in Peele's *Arraignment of Paris,*" *SP*, 65 (1968), 163–71.
26. Jonson's description of *Hymenaei*, in Orgel, *The Complete Masques*, p. 94.

Surcharged with the burden that she nill sustaine.
Th' unpartiall daughters of Necessitie
Bin aydes in her sute: and so the twine
That holdes olde Priams house, the threede of Troie
Dame Atropos with knife in sunder cuttes.
Done be the pleasure of the powers above,
Whose hestes men must obey: and I my parte
Performe in Ida vales . . .

To complain that this ought to, but does not, lead into a tragedy
of Troy and not a pastoral-mythological-complimentary comedy,
seems to me as irrelevant as it would be to berate Jonson for not
making a scene of "an ugly hell, which flaming beneath, smoked
unto the top of the roof" introduce a *Masque of Witches* rather
than the *Masque of Queens*. We cannot tell how striking Ate
looked, but her words are clearly meant to give a vivid image both
of the hell she comes from,

Where bloudles ghostes in paines of endles date
Fill ruthles eares with never ceasing cries,

and the hell the gods are going to create on earth:

Proude Troy must fall . . .
. . . .
King Priams pallace waste with flaming fire,
Whose thicke and foggie smoake piercing the skie,
Must serve for messenger of sacrifice
T'appeaze the anger of the angrie heavens.

The smoke and the cries give way to visual delight and musical
harmony as the scene becomes "Ida vales," but they remain, as it
were, in the periphery, as a sense of a world of discord elsewhere
– and one which, so "Th'unpartiall daughters of Necessitie" have
decreed, will eventually and inevitably take over. This sense is
underpinned by the extraordinary amount of sadness in the Arca-
dian world of the play. By the final scene, Colin has been carried
out on a bier, dead from a broken heart; Oenone, though still alive,
has lamented and left (and, as Peele well knew, the two lyrics of
lament are emotional centres of the play); and Paris, in a very
moving exit, has left the stage as "the shepherd boye /That in his
bosome carries fire to Troy." Now would seem the time for the

world of discord to take over; the wonder (not the structural defect) is that it does not. Its rulers are there, including "th'unpartiall dames of destenie" (as Clotho now describes them) who have materialized from Ate's Prologue; but even the Fates are wearing "robes of cheerfull collours," and they are there only to submit to the real ruler, the Queen. There must have been a shock to the audience as she entered the action – as essential to the play as is the visual shock when Hermione's statue "comes alive" in *The Winter's Tale.*

The theatrical climax (and the real denouement) is not the goddesses' argued decision to present the apple to Elizabeth because she is "so wise and fayre," but the ritual of submission which bounces us into acceptance of the mysterious power of royalty. The entry of the Fates is carefully prepared by music –

> *The Musicke sounde and the Nimphes within singe or solfa with voyces and instruments awhile. Then enter Clotho, Lachesis and Atropos singing as followeth: The state being in place*

and staged as a kind of sung Eucharist, the relative unfamiliarity of the Latin adding to the sense of wonder. As they lay their fatal instruments at the queen's feet, they might simply be pageant figures whose lines illustrate an emblematic gesture:

> Dame Atropos according as her pheeres
> To thee fayre Queene resignes her fatall knife,

but in the full structural context, with the Queen *there* and with the knife of Atropos having hovered over the action since the Prologue, they become a dramatic image of monarchy rising above the powers of fate and time. We are not in the dreamlike world of relative time which surrounds the figure of the Queen in *Endimion* but much more in the kind of unquestioned double time to which the English theatre had been used in the days of the *Secunda Pastorum.* Even as Mac is tossed in a blanket, the shepherds turn to God's Lamb in the manger. Even as Paris goes to start the Troyan war, according to "the pleasure of the powers above/ Whose hestes men must obey" (Prologue), the Queen rises above those powers. There is indeed a jolt in the final scene,[27] and the

27. As Enid Welsford complains, in *The Court Masque* (Cambridge, 1927), p. 281.

jolt itself is essential. The Queen is not just a super shepherdess, or the most beautiful and wise lady ever, as the language tells us. She is, as the whole visual-verbal-musical structure of the ending shows us, *different*, part of a mystery beyond possibility. The wonder of monarchy, Peele knew, would not make a play for the public stage; but, as *Tamburlaine* and possibly *The Spanish Tragedy* had just demonstrated, tyranny would. It is easy enough to be scathing about *The Battle of Alcazar*, for in Peele's attempt to dramatize the workings of political evil there is so much that seemed absurd even to his contemporaries. The exiled and starving tyrant enters "*with [raw] flesh upon his sword*"; and the unintentional parody of a Tamburlaine rhapsody which follows was in its turn parodied by Shakespeare and many others:

> Hold thee Calypolis feed and faint no more,
>
> . . . .
>
> Feede then and faint not faire Calypolis. (ll. 537–61)

There is so much, too, that could have been in the play but is not. The nearly contemporary historical events which form the plot contain a number of interesting moral paradoxes: a justified ruler who yet had to make his way to the throne by violence, in Abdelmelec; a usurping ruler driven into exile, where he has some cause for feeling more sinned against than sinning, in Muly Mahamet; a good king, misled and forced into the position of a villain, in Sebastian of Portugal, and so on. But Peele does not have the language for moral discriminations which in Shakespeare's histories illuminates and patterns similar raw material. The most that he manages is a heavy-handed insistence on the essential innocence of Sebastian, and his misfortune of getting mixed up, together with the protean Stukeley, in the African venture. Nor can his imagination do much (apart from some spectacular scenes of battle or of triumphant entry, and from the eulogy of Queen Elizabeth and her nation put into the mouth of Sebastian) to transmute the factual material. The historical-political scene tends to be rendered with the prosaic dispassionateness of a news announcer, as in the following account of Sebastian's progress towards the scene of the battle:

> The 26. daie of June he left the bay of Lisborne,
> And with all his fleete at Cardis happily he

Arriv'de in Spain the eight of July, tarrying for the aide
That Philip king of Spaine had promised,
And fifteene daies he there remaind aboord. (ll. 883–7)

If then the historical plot as such did not fire Peele's imagination, what did was the general, ineluctable sense of retribution taking its course which he could derive from the plot and both "show" and discuss in the dumb-shows and the Presenter's speeches. The transition from the general vision to the particular situation often has the sinking effect of a "Tey Bridge Disaster," as in the dumb-show before the last act and the Presenter's comment,

The crownes of Barbary and kingdomes fall,
Ay me, that kingdomes may not stable stand,
And now approching neere the dismall day,
The bloudie daie wherein the battels joyne,
Mondaie the fourth of August seventie eight. (ll. 1180–4)

In other words, if the language of the play is constantly letting us down, the imaginative core of the play is the framework of dumb-shows which show us how evil deeds set in motion an infernal machinery.

Because the 1594 Quarto represents such an imperfect and abbreviated version of the play, it has been difficult to get any sort of overall sense of its original structure. In the Quarto there is no trace of the third dumb-show, for example, and scarcely more than fragments of the second and the fourth. But W. W. Greg's invaluable edition of the theatrical plot of *The Battle of Alcazar*, and now also the heroic labours of the Yale editor, John Yoklavich, who sensibly incorporates information from the "plot" into the stage directions he prints, indicate that Peele is using the dumb-shows as a consistent fatalistic framework.[28] The real structure of the play is an overall visual pattern.

From the audience's point of view, the chief character in this play is the Presenter. Unlike Revenge in *The Spanish Tragedy*, who together with the Ghost of Andrea makes up a self-contained audience *within* the play, he maintains a very immediate relationship with us "lords" or "lordinges." This is established in his speech which opens the play,

28. Greg, *Two Elizabethan Stage Abridgements*, and Yoklavich, ed., *The Battle of Alcazar*, vol. 2 of the Yale edition.

> Sit you and see this true and tragicke warr
> A modern matter full of bloud and ruth (ll. 49–50)

and he makes no bones about the *de casibus* nature of this "modern matter":

> Where three bolde kings confounded in their height,
> Fall to the earth contending for a crowne. (ll. 51–2)

At the same time he is flexible in his approach to the matter he has to present. His first task is to provide a résumé of the action before the dramatic present: fifteen lines of exposition which, at first sight, are almost unintelligible to a reader, because of the dynastic complications and because everybody seems to have the same name. But then the first dumb-show takes over and shows us, in three separate scenes, how Muly Mahamet and his son, together with two Murderers, strangle the two young princes in their bed, "in sight of the uncle" Abdelmunen, and then proceed to strangle this unfortunate spectator in his chair. While we still measure the length of plays in numbers of lines instead of hours of traffic on the stage, it is worth reminding ourselves how long this would have taken to show – and, incidentally, how after this no one in the audience need be confused about which Muly Mahamet is which. At this stage, the Presenter's commentary is, if sensational, as directly related to what we see as that of a lantern slide lecturer:

> this tyrant king,
> Of whome we treate sprong from the Arabian moore
> Blacke in his looke, and bloudie in his deeds,
> And in his shirt staind with a cloud of gore,
> Presents himselfe with naked sword in hand,
> Accompanied as now you may behold,
> With devils coted in the shapes of men. (ll. 14–20)

All the more effectively, therefore, he can warn us, at the end of this first dumb-show, against brushing aside what we see as mere fiction – "Saie not these things are faind, for true they are" – and also relate what we have seen to the universal pattern of "Nemesis high mistres of revenge." Then, at last, he can turn to the actual present of the play. His "now behold" introduces the first scene of the play proper, so that there is, at this stage in the play, no distinction felt between dumb-show and speaking show.

The first dumb-show, then, shows nothing which has not happened in real life. But, as the action progresses, the dumb-shows come more and more to be of another world (one hesitates to use as presumptuous a phrase as "another level of reality"): their cast includes supernatural powers and their "plots" become increasingly allegorical. Nemesis, "*three ghosts crying* Vindicta" and three Furies appear at the beginning of Act II. In the third show we see the pulsations of unmerited pain as the innocent and misled are drawn into the infernal machine. At the beginning of Act IV Sebastian and Stukeley feast with the Moor, at "the bloudie banquet," on dead men's heads and similar delicacies. And the last dumb-show, of lightning and thunder, blazing stars and fireworks and the fall of two crowns from the tree where "Fame like an Angel" has deposited them, completes the allegorization of the "modern matter" into the *de casibus* pattern initially outlined by the Presenter. There is an interesting enjambement here, between the end of Act IV and the opening of Act V, for the dumb-show comes as an ironic visual response to the Moor's attempt to invoke "You bastards of the night, and Erybus,/ Fiends, Fairies, hags . . ." (ll. 1136–7), and to prescribe (like the Ghost of Andrea at the end of *The Spanish Tragedy*, but unsuccessfully) a detailed set of hellish punishments for his enemies.

It is as if Peele was beginning to feel his way towards counterpointing word and show, rather than merely having one illustrate the other – a way which, however remotely, leads towards the irony when Macbeth's assurance that Banquo, like all mortals, is "assailable" is translated, in the banquet scene, to the visual certainty that the dead "now . . . rise again." It is that sense of the mystery of evil which occasionally makes *The Battle of Alcazar* rise above cliché or parody; and, to me, the most undeniable of such occasions rests in the combination of language and visual effects around the dumb-show of Act II. The Presenter introduces Nemesis and goes on to say:

> Nor may the silence of the speechlesse night,
> Divine Architect of murthers and misdeeds,
> Of tragedies and tragicke tyrannies,
> Hide or containe this barbarous crueltie
> Of this usurper to his progenie. (ll. 279–83)

On the page, it looks like the kind of verbal statement about night (like Lucrece's outcry to "comfort-killing Night, image of Hell! . . . Black stage for tragedies and murders fell!" [ll. 764–6]) which the literature of the period teems with. But night here really becomes identified with the "black stage," as the theatre situation makes manifest, through eyes and ears, the ghastly nature – the relentless irony – of "the silence of the speechlesse night." (Three ghosts crying "Vindicta" might not look so funny on stage as they do in the study.) If silk purses were ever made of sows' ears, one would suggest that there is a germ of *Macbeth* here, in the confrontation with the infernal machinery set in motion by, and therefore ironically working against, the "Traitor to kinne and kinde, to Gods and men" (*Alcazar*, l. 287). The wonder of evil is epitomized in the night which, in a hallucinatory way, both facilitates deeds and brings about retribution for them.

Whatever *The Battle of Alcazar* achieves, it suggests that glories rather than horrors are Peele's forte. A sense of this may be the reason why, in his attempt at an English history play, he turned to a king who started in the triumph of victorious Holy Wars and went on, through encounters with a Welsh Greenwood world, to the glory of national unity, and who, besides, was a great lover. I am prepared to accept the persuasive argument of the Yale editor of *Edward I*, Frank S. Hook, that the parts of the play vilifying Queen Elinor were interpolations, to accommodate the contents of the two ballads on "The lamentable fall of Queene Elnor" and "Queen Eleanor's Confession."[29] There are absurdities in these parts – like the wonder of the Queen sinking into the earth on Charing Green and popping up again at Potters Hive – which seem like (but are not) deliberate parodies on "wonder." There are other textual problems, dealt with by Hook, which I cannot go into here. But if, through these complications, we try to glimpse the original and unrevised structure of the play, we find it to be, like that of *The Battle of Alcazar*, a primarily visual one. The action moves through a series of pageants: the triumphal entry at the beginning, the coronation of Edward, the (dumb-show) christening of the Prince of Wales and wedding of Jone and Gloster, followed by revels (laconically referred to in the stage

29. See vol. 2 of the Yale edition, pp. 19–37.

direction as "the showe": l. 1964). And, though we do not reach Elinor's funeral, Edward's lament for her death is itself soon deflected into an envisaged celebration:

> You peeres of England, see in roiall pompe,
> These breathles bodies be entombed straight,
> With tried colours covered all with blacke,
> Let Spanish steedes as swift as fleeting winde,
> Convaie these Princes to their funerall,
> Before them let a hundred mourners ride . . . (ll. 2630–5)

Suitably (in terms of the structure, rather than the character), the last reference to Elinor is a sort of apotheosis, as Edward orders

> a rich and statelie carved Crosse,
> Whereon her stature shall with glorie shine. (ll. 2642–3)

Suitably, too, even after the revisions the play ends as a kind of speaking show: Gloster alone on stage with the dead body of Jone, giving us a *Klagerede* in which the language draws attention to what is seen: "Thy eies thy lookes thy lippes and everie part" (l. 2674).

The revision theory clearly does not account for all the oddities and unevennesses of the play. After the single-mindedness of *The Battle of Alcazar*, *Edward I* provides a Greene-like hotch-potch of emotions. Yet there are moments when the play seems to pull itself together into amazing anticipations of dramatic and poetic modes to come. The finest of these is in the coronation scene, in what the text proudly marks out as "*Queene Elinors speeche.*" Its qualities are such that I cannot believe the Yale editor when he puts it down as another "Spanish pride" interpolation; nor can I agree with him that "it is so extravagant that it verges at times on nonsense."[30] It is necessary to quote the speech in full:

> The welken spangled through with goulden spots,
> Reflects no finer in a frostie night,
> Then lovely Longshankes in his Elinors eye:
> So Ned thy Nell in every part of thee,
> Thy person's garded with a troope of Queenes,
> And every Queene as brave as Elinor,

30. Ibid., p. 182 (note on ll. 704 ff.).

Gives glorie to these glorious christall quarries,
Where every orbe an object entertaines,
Of riche device and princelie majestie.
Thus like Narcissus diving in the deepe,
I die in honour and in Englands armes:
And if I drowne, it is in my delight,
Whose companie is cheefest life in death,
From forth whose currall lips I suck the sweete,
Wherewith are daintie Cupids caudles made,
Then live or die brave Ned, or sinke or swim,
An earthlie blisse it is to looke on him.
On thee sweete Ned, it shall become thy Nell,
Bounteous to be unto the beauteous,
Ore prie the palmes sweete fountaines of my blisse,
And I will stand on tiptoe for a kisse. (ll. 704–24)

Well may we ask "What words, what looks, what wonders?"
What is remarkable about this speech is, first, the interaction of
words and looks and, second, the way the wonder is being experienced by the audience *through* the speaker. By this second
point I do not so much mean that it is a characterizing, differ-
entiating, speech (in the same play Lluellen, for one, speaks in a
very similar tone, with similar vocabulary and imagery, when he
sets eyes on *his* Elinor) as that we wonder with and at a human
experience, not at a dramatic situation or concept, as we did in
Peele's earlier plays. By the first, I mean the remarkable way in
which visual excitement generates verbal excitement and *vice
versa*. It is not the remembered visual excitement of Enobarbus in
his barge speech, but an actual visual presence in which the
audience shares; not the one-sided rapt description of Iachimo as
he watches the sleeping Imogen, but a rapt mutuality, where love
and self-love merge, strangely anticipating both sentiment and
imagery in a poem like Donne's "Good-Morrow" or his "Sun
Rising." While the verbal imagery arises out of the visual situation,
part of the wonder, as in a metaphysical poem, lies in the very
ingenuity of the verbal conceits; for example, Elinor, losing herself
in Edward's embrace, is like Narcissus drowning in his mirroring
pool. But she dies, as the lovers die in "The Canonization," in two
senses; and presumably "in England's armes" is a double image,
too. Because the speech is set in a very public context, the raptness
(as in Antony and Cleopatra's first dialogue) is tempered by self-

consciousness; the tones of private love-making mingle with those of public demonstration. There is no description as such; every twist of the eulogistic argument, every new conceit, arises out of the stage situation of the newly crowned and glass-suited monarch and, in turn, modifies our apprehension of that situation – right through to the last line, which is both a touching climax to the imagery and a stage direction ("And I will stand on tiptoe for a kisse"). That line, with its concrete reference to the problems of kissing the tall King, also brings to rest the remarkable balancing in the speech, between homely Ned Longshanks and glorious "England," between Nell (the persona who, elsewhere in the play, like a true Mrs. Bagnet, will tuck up her skirts and follow her man to the wars) and brave Queen Elinor. Again, for a moment, Peele is capable of hinting at a range of ruler-lover relationships that looks forward to *Antony and Cleopatra*.

In talking about the visual situation, I am, of course, above all referring to the "sute of Glasse" which Edward is wearing. It seems to have been a precious piece of property of the Admiral's Men.[31] Elinor, in the first scene, builds up our expectations of the coronation scene mainly around this suit and the wonderful tableau it will create, again one in which majesty and love, adoration and narcissism, meet:

> My King like Phoebus bridegroom like shall marche
> With lovely Thetis to her glassie bed,
> And all the lookers on shall stand amazde,
> To see King Edward and his lovely Queene,
> Sit lovely in Englands stately throne. (ll. 263–7)

With all this pre-release publicity – and, if Hook is right in inserting the Quarto's three misplaced lines,

> And lovelie England to thy lovely Queene,
> Lovelie Queene Elinor, unto her turne thy eye,
> Whose honor cannot but love thee wel,

immediately before "Queene Elinors speeche," with a tremendous claim in the actual credit titles – the scene might easily have

---

31. It is generally accepted that this was the "longeshanckes sewte" which Henslowe records as "gone and loste" in an inventory taken on 10 March 1598, but which was found and listed in another inventory, three days later. (See ibid., p. 7.)

seemed anticlimactic. But, whatever the glass suit actually looked like, it is what we see of it through the language that matters: its power of many-faceted reflections. Edward is reflected in her eyes and she in every one of the crystal mirrors that make up the suit; and as we follow the breathless path of the conceits, the two become an image of majesty in love. She is in love with him *as* King, with the King's two bodies at once: "I die in honour and in Englands armes."

I make no claims for *Edward I* as a whole, merely for the raptness of occasional moments like this. Such raptness is much more prominent in *David and Bethsabe*. By the time he had written *Edward I*, Peele had, however fitfully, explored the wonder of monarchy, of evil and retribution, and of the king as lover. We do not know how he came to make the unusual choice of a biblical subject for his (presumably) next and last play. But it is an almost too neat conclusion to my quest that he should have chosen a king who was also both a lover and a penitent sinner, and a divine poet. I do not think Peele was aware of any such neat pattern to his career; but he must have been aware of writing a highly ambitious play. Wonder surrounds the hero and the subject by definition. It is articulated into a proto-Miltonic epic invocation by the Prologue, and it becomes the basic informing principle behind the verbal texture as well as the dramatic structure. In the language it comes out as a desire to load every rift with ore (except when, as in Nathan's parable, Peele follows the Bible almost verbatim), so that the heroic or amorous passages shine with celestial lights or sparkle with jewels, while the passages of sin and dejection are dark and horrid in the extreme. There is always a tendency for Peele's imagery to move between the two extremes of the entrails of the earth and the "lamp of heaven"; and here this tendency – contrasting the two extremes, or moving from one to the other – becomes in itself an organizing structural pattern.

But before we turn to the structure of *David and Bethsabe*, it is worth noting how much the play and its poetry are concerned with seeing. Characters are constantly telling us about the visual impressions they make upon each other, and usually they do so in an elaborate simile which, as it were, turns the interlocutor (whom we see on stage) into a wondrous picture. David exquisitely records how the eye and the desires of the beholder modify the beheld:

> Now comes my lover tripping like the Roe,
> And brings my longings tangled in her haire. (ll. 115–6)

Ammon addresses Absalon (who, ironically, is about to kill him) as "Thou faire young man, whose haires shine in mine eye/ Like golden wyers of Davids yvorie Lute" (ll. 747–8). And, in a famous set passage, Joab turns David's presence on stage into a pageant of the sun king:

> Beauteous and bright is he among the Tribes,
> As when the sunne attir'd in glist'ring robe,
> Comes dauncing from his orientall gate,
> And bridegroome-like hurles through the gloomy aire
> His radiant beames, *such doth King David shew,*
> Crownd with the honour of his enemies towne,
> Shining in riches like the firmament,
> The starrie vault that overhangs the earth,
> *So looketh David King of Israel.* (ll. 825–33; my italics)

There is a connection in the play between the characters' interest in how they see each other and the pervading sense that God sees them all. Characters repeatedly describe themselves as if in the sight of God. Absalon in his *hubris* sees his own beauty as a kind of election:

> Absalon, that in his face
> Carries the finall purpose of his God,
>
> . . . .
>
> His thunder is intangled in my haire,
> And with my beautie is his lightning quencht,
> I am the man he made to glorie in. (ll. 1163–71)

David, on the other hand, sees his own sins as "printed in his browes." What God sees makes up the universe of the play, both in space and time. Like Milton's God, he has "before [his] eyes" all human actions "From Adam to the end of Adams seed" (ll. 1740–1). And, like Milton's Adam, Peele's Solomon has to be warned against presumptuous attempts to see too much with merely human eyes:

> Wade not too farre my boy in waves too deepe.
> The feeble eyes of our aspiring thoughts
> Behold things present and record things past:

> But things to come, exceed our humane reach,
> And are not painted yet in angels eyes. (ll. 1726–9)

It is true that the last two examples come from a scene where Peele is engaged in wholesale borrowing from Du Bartas' *Les Artifices*; but, as I have tried to show elsewhere,[32] this scene is thematically very central in Peele's play. It is notable, too, that the evocative references to vision, human and superhuman, are Peele's own; Du Bartas "l'oeil de nostre pensée" becomes "the feeble eyes of our aspiring thoughts," and "not painted yet in angels eyes" is all Peele.

The sense that what we are watching on stage is happening in the eyes of God gives peculiar poignancy to the hero's moral progress. David knows that God "sees our hearts" (l. 993), and he discovers that, through contrition, it is possible to "find favour in his gratious eyes" (l. 1055). And the mark of God's grace is a new vision:

> vertue to mine eies,
> To tast the comforts, and behold the forme
> Of his faire arke, and holy tabernacle. (ll. 1058–60)

It cannot be fortuitous, then, that the play opens on a human vision and closes on a divine: that it moves from David "above" viewing Bethsabe to David below, imagining for his dead son the beatific moment when "Thou shalt behold thy soveraigne face to face" (l. 1914).

Some time ago now, I tried to analyse the structure of *David and Bethsabe* and to show how, though infinitely less articulate than *Paradise Lost*, Peele's play yet anticipates Milton's epic on the Fall and the Redemption.[33] In what I have just said, I am trying to suggest that Peele was using all the resources of the theatre to put across the wonder of falling and rising in the eyes of God. We see this more clearly, perhaps, if we notice how persistently the fall/rise structure of the play as a whole is repeated within the individual scenes, or within a pair of contiguous scenes. Sometimes the local pattern is of rise/fall, as when the virtual apotheosis of David victorious on the walls of Rabba is im-

---

32. "The House of David," p. 37. For Peele's borrowings from Du Bartas, see P. H. Cheffaud, *George Peele* (Paris, 1913), esp. p. 131; and H. D. Sykes, "Peele's Borrowings from Du Bartas," *NQ*, CXLVII (1924), 349–51, 368–9.
33. "The House of David," esp. p. 39.

mediately followed by the announcement that all his sons are dead. Often one character rises as another falls. But in all these cases, the movement is pointed by the visual stage image as well as by the verbal imagery. As Absalon usurps David's throne, David's dejection –

> *Enter David . . . with others, David barefoot, with some lose covering over his head, and all mourning;* (l. 972 SD)
>
> *He lies downe and all the rest after him* (l. 991 SD)

– and the ritual scene of lamentation which translates it into words, are followed by the entry of

> *Absalon . . . with the concubines of David, and others in great state, Absalon crowned* (l. 1106 SD),

and by a speech from Absalon in which he contrasts his own sun-and-star-like glory with David "whose life is with his honour fast inclosd/Within the entrailes of a Jeatie cloud" (ll. 1107 ff.).

But the most significant fall/rise scenes conern David alone and take him from prostration to some form of celebration or, in moral terms, from sin to awareness of grace. The scene of Nathan's parable is perhaps the best example. David's speech of repentance –

> Nathan, have against the Lord, I have
> Sinned, O sinned grievously, and loe
> From heavens throne doth David throw himselfe,
> And grone and grovell to the gates of hell.
> *He fals downe* (ll. 656-9 SD)

– is unmemorable as poetry but interesting as marking a truly emblematic stage situation. The speech explains what is seen, turning the stage itself into a moral map, a space between heaven and hell.[34] As the death of the child of sin is announced, the fact that this means, in David's morality, not only judgment but also absolution is brought home in visual language:

34. In later, more "realistic" drama, stage space can still be a moral measure: as when Isabella in *Women Beware Women*, having learnt that her uncle is after all her uncle, exclaims: "In that small distance from yon man to me/Lies sin enough to make a whole world perish" – the distance being both in blood and what the audience can see. (*Women Beware Women*, IV.ii. 131–2; ed. Roma Gill, London, 1968).

They bring in water, wine, and oyle. Musike, and a banquet.
They use all solemnities together, and sing, etc.

(ll. 712 SD and 716 SD)

David's words, on the other hand, are also taken up with the
symbolical import of his redemption:

> And decke faire Bersabe with ornaments,
> That she may bear to me another sonne. (ll. 708–9)

The last scene of the play is built on the same pattern. It begins
with David's prostration at the death of Absalon (he *"sits close"*
and Bethsabe *"kneeles downe"*) and leads to a reversal where
David *"riseth up"* and, in a speech of spiritual renewal, envisages
the beatitude of Absalon. But, instead of resorting to the external-
ized pattern of the scene just analysed, Peele is here trying to work
from inside David's experience, which means he has to rely almost
entirely on language. Absalon is to David here rather like Lycidas
(i.e. King) to Milton; it is not really the dead man's fate that
matters, but the spiritual state of the speaker. Absalon's rising to
heaven, where he will truly become that celestial light which both
he and David have constantly been compared to –

> Thy eyes now no more eyes but shining stars,
> Shall decke the flaming heavens with novell lampes (ll. 1908–9)

– marks David's redemption. And finally the wonder of a transfigured vision bursts upon us:

> and the curtaine drawne,
> Thou shalt behold thy soveraigne face to face,
> With wonder knit in triple unitie,
> Unitie infinite and innumerable. (ll. 1913–16)

Peele took the image which introduces the vision, "the curtaine
drawne," straight from Du Bartas ("la courtine tirée"), but I cannot believe that he was unaware how it echoed his opening stage
direction (*"He drawes a curtaine, and discovers Bethsabe . . ."*).
The play's last and greatest wonder is presented, within language,
as a theatrical "discovery."

Peele did not have the ability to realize characters and construct
a dramatic scene where, as in the final scene of *The Winter's Tale*,

153

silence carries the wonder of the impossible becoming possible. No more than Milton did he have a language for the mystic vision; and like Milton he tries to express the inexpressible through abstract nouns and negative adjectives: "Unitie infinite and innumerable." But if the play's climax, then, is a failure – a wonder talked about rather than realized – it is the kind of failure which demands respect, and to which attention must be paid. In its attempt to use biblical history to dramatize something of the wonder of sin and redemption, of death and renewal, *David and Bethsabe* is a link between the Mysteries and Shakespeare's last plays. And it is so because, throughout his career, Peele is ready to experiment with words, looks and wonders.

The Contributors

DAVID BEVINGTON, Professor of English, University of Chicago. Author of *From "Mankind" to Marlowe, Tudor Drama and Politics* and numerous articles on Shakespeare and Elizabethan drama.

T. W. CRAIK, Professor of English, University of Dundee. Author of *The Tudor Interlude, The Comic Tales of Chaucer* and numerous articles on Shakespeare and Elizabethan drama.

INGA-STINA EWBANK, Reader in English Literature, Bedford College, University of London. Author of *Their Proper Sphere: A Study of the Brontë Sisters as Early Victorian Female Novelists* and numerous articles on Shakespeare, Elizabethan drama and Ibsen.

R. W. INGRAM, Professor of English, University of British Columbia. Author of "Music as Structural Element in Shakespeare" and other articles on Shakespeare and Elizabethan drama.

D. F. ROWAN, Professor of English, University of New Brunswick. Author of "The Cockpit-in-Court" and other articles on the Elizabethan stage and Elizabethan drama.

PETER SACCIO, Professor of English, Dartmouth College. Author of *The Court Comedies of John Lyly: A Study in Allegorical Dramaturgy* and articles on Elizabethan drama.

J. A. B. SOMERSET, Professor of English, University of Western Ontario. Author of "New Facts Concerning Samuel Rowley" and other articles on Elizabethan drama.

RICHARD SOUTHERN, sometime Lecturer in Drama and Theatre Architecture, University of Bristol. Author of *Changeable Scenery, The Mediaeval Theatre in the Round, The Staging of Plays before Shakespeare* and other books on the theatre.

Index

Index

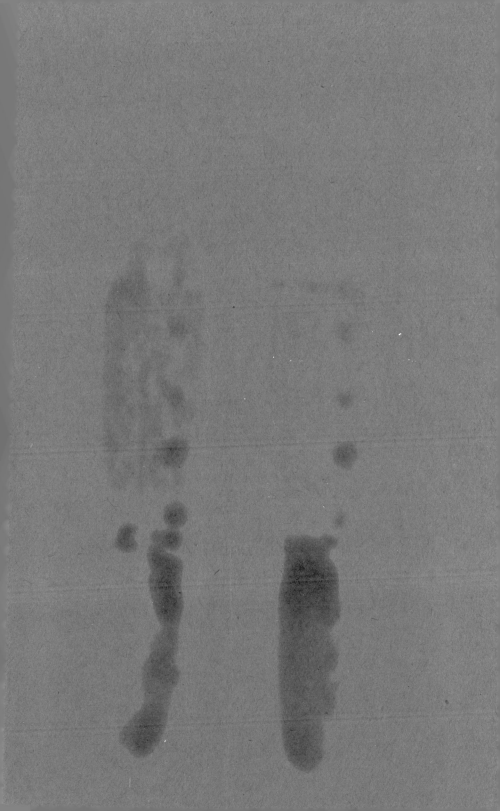

80171

INTERNATIONAL CONFERENCE ON ELIZA-
BETHAN THEATRE